the
only
    dance
there is

RAM DASS was born Richard Alpert in 1931 in Boston. He received a Ph.D. in psychology from Stanford University in 1957 and taught at Stanford, the University of California at Berkeley, and Harvard University, where he researched in the fields of human motivation, Freudian theories of early social development, cognition, and clinical pathology.

Dr. Alpert first ingested psilocybin in 1961. Soon after, he joined with Timothy Leary and others in a research program concerning altered states of consciousness brought about through the use of psychedelics. Using his training in psychology, he observed a psychodynamic shift in himself but ultimately found the psychedelically induced experience was limited.

In 1967 Dr. Alpert journeyed to India, searching for the source of the wisdom he had read about in Eastern religious texts. Several months later he settled at a tiny temple in the Himalayas for a winter of study under the direction of Neem Karoli Baba, his guru. In 1968 he returned with the name Ram Dass (given to him by Baba) to pursue his *sadhana* (spiritual journey) in the West.

Ram Dass authored the classic *Be Here Now*, which sold nearly a million copies and profoundly shaped the Western spiritual awakening that emerged in the early seventies; *Miracle of Love*, which recounts the stories of those whose lives were transformed by the late Neem Karoli Baba; and *How Can I Help*, his most recent work, which examines the spiritual role of service and the issues that confront those who choose a path of compassionate action.

Besides his books and articles, Ram Dass helped form and continues to participate in the Seva Foundation, a national and international service group. He is on the board of directors of Creating Our Future, and organization to foster the political empowerment of teenagers, and he helps the terminally ill use the processes of dying as an opportunity for spiritual unfoldment. Ram Dass shares his teachings through retreats, workshops, and lectures, and continues to deepen his own awareness through meditation and study.

I have been in that heaven, the most illumined by light from him and seen things which to utter, he who returns hath neither skill nor knowledge, for as it nears the object of its yearning our intellect is overwhelmed so deeply it can never retrace the path that it followed. But whatsoever of the holy kingdom was in the power of memory to treasure, it will be my theme until the song is ended.

DANTE

Swiftly arose and spread around me the place, the peace and joy and knowledge that passes all the art and argument of the earth, and I know that the hand of God is the elder hand of my own, and I know that the Spirit is the eldest brother of my own, and that all men ever born are also my brothers and the women my sisters and lovers, and that a kelson of creation is love.

WALT WHITMAN

Truth lies within ourselves; it takes no rise from outward things, whate'er you may believe. There is an inmost center in us all, where truth abides in fullness and to know rather consists in opening out a way whence the imprisoned splendor may escape than in effecting entry for light supposed to be without.

ROBERT BROWNING

A man is the facade of a temple wherein all wisdom and all good abide. What we commonly call man, the eating, drinking, counting, planting man, does not as we know him represent himself, but misrepresents himself.

RALPH WALDO EMERSON

RAM
DASS

the only dance there is

Talks Given at the Menninger Foundation,
Topeka, Kansas, 1970,
and at Spring Grove Hospital,
Spring Grove, Maryland, 1972.

ANCHOR BOOKS
DOUBLEDAY
NEW YORK LONDON TORONTO SYDNEY AUCKLAND

AN ANCHOR BOOK

PUBLISHED BY DOUBLEDAY

a division of Bantam Doubleday Dell Publishing Group, Inc.
1540 Broadway, New York, New York 10036

ANCHOR BOOKS, DOUBLEDAY, and the portrayal of an anchor
are trademarks of Doubleday, a division of Bantam Doubleday
Dell Publishing Group, Inc.

All four parts of *The Only Dance There Is* have been published
in slightly different form in the *Journal of Transpersonal Psychology*.
The Anchor Books edition is published by arrangement with
the Transpersonal Institute.

DESIGNED BY WILMA ROBIN

ISBN 0-385-08413-7

Library of Congress Catalog Card Number 73-14054

This book came into being in steps. Ram Dass gave a lecture to a group of health sciences professionals in Topeka, Kansas, in 1970. After it was taped, it seemed desirable to make it more available. It was transcribed and the lecture was published in two issues of the *Journal of Transpersonal Psychology* in 1970 and 1971. We felt that Ram Dass's amalgam of Western training and Eastern experiences would be highly valuable to our readers. Their response from the beginning has been very gratifying.

In 1972 Ram Dass gave a different lecture to another professional group at Spring Grove State Hospital in Baltimore. We were sent the tape and given permission to transcribe, edit, and print the lecture. Again response was so impressive that we decided both lectures should be made available to a wider public. Doubleday agreed to publish them in the present volume, thus assuring a comprehensive distribution at a reasonable cost to the reader.

Historically, one spiritual system after another has been assimilated in another culture in such a way as to modify the form of the discipline without diminishing its essence. In this respect, Ram Dass has been especially effective in helping Americans and other Westerners feel "at home" in what has been considered a "foreign" tradition.

The Editorial Staff and Board of Editors are deeply grateful to Ram Dass for having given us permission to publish these lectures and for his generosity in turning over all royalties to the *Journal of Transpersonal Psychology*.

ANTHONY J. SUTICH, Editor, and
JAMES FADIMAN, Associate Editor,
Journal of Transpersonal Psychology

the
only
dance
there is

one

The Path of Consciousness

Last evening, here in Topeka, as one of the journeyers on a
path, a very, very old path, the path of consciousness, I, in a
sense, met with the Explorers Club to tell about the geography
I had been mapping. The people who gather to hear somebody
called Ram Dass, formerly Richard Alpert, have somewhere,
at some level, in some remote corner, some involvement
in this journey. All that I can see that we can do with one
another is share notes of our exploration. I can say, "Watch
out, because around that bend the road falls off sharply to the
left . . . stay far over on the right when you do that."

The motivation for doing this is most interesting—it's only
to work on myself. It's very easy to break attachments to worldly
games when you're sitting in a cave in the Himalayas. It's
quite a different take you do of sex, power, money, fame, and
sensual gratification in the middle of New York City in the
United States with television and loving people around and
great cooks and advertising and total support for all of the
attachments. But there is the story of a monk who got very
holy up on the mountain until he had some thousands of
followers. After many years he went down into a city and he
was in the town and somebody jostled him. He turned around
angrily and that anger was a mark of how little work he had
really done on himself. For all the work he had done he still
hadn't clipped the seed of anger; he still got uptight when
somebody pushed him around.

So that what I see as my own *sadhana* (my work on my own

1

consciousness—it could also be called my spiritual journey) is that it is very much cyclic. There are periods of going out and there are periods of turning back in, periods of going out and periods of going back in. Just as living here in the market place is forcing things into the forefront, so sitting in a room by myself for 30 or 40 days in a mountain is forcing other things to be confronted. Each hides from the other, each environment hides from the other sets of stimulus conditions. For example, in the commune we've been designing up in the mountains of New Mexico, where I ran an ashram for awhile this winter, the design has four components to it which are roughly related to the solstices.

The Four Component Design of Ashram

For one period, a person would be in the hermitage on the top of the hill where he would be going deep—diving deep within. He would be totally alone in solitude in a hermitage. The food is left outside the door. In the one I ran this winter, the people would go in for up to nineteen days. The first time they went in I let them take books and pictures and weaving and all of their things (their pet kind of cream cheese or whatever it was they needed). For the second round we changed the game a little and all they took in was their sleeping bag. They walked into a room, closed the door, and for the next ten days, fire and wood and food were left outside and there was a jug of water. They were all protected, all taken care of. There were no phones to answer, no mail. We were protecting them and giving them that chance to get free of all the stimuli that keep capturing consciousness all the time so that one keeps saying, "If it weren't for . . ." Well, we did that. We created that place.

A second part of the four-point cycle is that a person *lives* in a commune, an ashramite lives in the commune . . . that is, he takes care of the gardens, the babies, the goats, cooks the food, chops the wood, does Karma Yoga. That is, Karma Yoga among what's called *satsang* or *sangha*, that is, a com-

2

munity of other beings who consciously know they are working on their own consciousness. In Buddhism there is a traditional thing you do which is to take the three refuges. There is a chant, which means, first, "I take refuge in the Buddha," I take refuge in the fact that a being can become enlightened, that is, a being can get free of any particular state of consciousness (attachment). Second, "I take refuge in the Dharma," I take refuge in the law, in the organization of the universe, the laws of the universe, you can also call it karma. And third, "I take refuge in the Sangha," in the community of other people, of monks on the path, the community of other people who are seeking. Thus, when you define yourself as a seeker after sensual gratification then you surround yourself with other people who are seekers after sensual gratification. When you define yourself as an intellectual you often surround yourself with intellectuals. When you define yourself as a seeker after consciousness, you start to surround yourself with other seekers after consciousness, because in that phase being around such people really gives you a kind of environmental support.

What I mean by the word consecration is bringing into consciousness the nature of the act in a cosmic plan. For example, in the old days people would say grace. Grace was a thing you waited for before you ate the turkey. Norman Rockwell characterizes the kid reaching while everybody's head's bowed. It's that time, "Let's say grace." "Grace." Now, when I bless food, the statement I say, when I say grace, is an old Sanskrit one. It means "This offering of this little ritual I'm performing, this is part of it all, part of Brahma, part of that which is eternally all. He who is making the offering means, that which is being offered is part of it all. The hunger to which you are feeding . . . the fire which you are feeding, that's all part of it all. Whoever you are offering it to is part of it all, too. He who realizes that all of it is interrelated, all of it is one, becomes one with it all."

There is a very lovely short story by J. D. Salinger called *Teddy*, in which Teddy is like an old lama who has taken a

3

reincarnation in a kind of middle class western family by some quirk of cosmic design. He is about ten years old and on a ship with his sister and his mother and father. He's out on deck and he is meeting this man who has begun to see that this little boy isn't quite like a little boy, and he says to him, "When did you first realize that you . . . how it was?" And Teddy says, "Well, I was 6 years old. I was in the kitchen and I was watching my little sister in her high-chair drink milk. I suddenly saw, that it was sort of like God pouring God into God, if you know what I mean." Well, that's exactly the same thing as that Sanskrit mantra. You're pouring energy into energy for a matter of energy in honoring energy. So big deal, so nothing's happened. Certainly knocks a hole in orality to start to see the universe that way. What are we doing? Nothing. How could you ever do anything, it's all here? Are we all here? Sure. So in learning how to consecrate and so on it is helpful to have people around.

It is part of my karma to be visiting my father who is a seventy-three-year-old Republican from Boston, a conservative man, and a very successful man in the society. When we sit down to the table, he starts to eat and then he looks over and he sees that I'm doing this "thing" which I do quietly. I'm not coming on about it, I'm just sort of sitting quietly . . . and he'll hold his spoon in mid-air and he'll go, "pht." It's almost an involuntary thing that comes out. It's like, "O.K., I'll wait for the kid . . . it's his *meshuggeneh* thing." Now that's not *satsang*, that is, that is not the community of monks on the path. And that "pht," whether that helps me or hinders me . . . is a function of where I'm at, really. In other words, if I am into what I'm doing strongly enough, all that that "pht" does is arouse a feeling of poignancy about our predicament, but it doesn't in any way deter from the amount of the living, vibrant quality I can invest in the thing I'm doing.

I go to church now and then around the United States and we sing hymns that are mind-blowers. They are all hymns that get you "high." They were written by people in ecstatic

4

states and you read them . . . everybody's singing them like they're reading the shopping list. There's no spirit, the spirit isn't invested in any way in the singing and yet whoever wrote it invested the spirit. We say, "Well, they were naive." What we mean is that *we* are turned off. When Christ says, "Look, I am making all things new," it's the same as when you're really living here and now and every moment is all fresh. It's like the first time you ever heard that hymn and you really go out on it. Otherwise, what did you go to church for?

The third part of the ashram cycle is where a member of the community goes into the city, society, and pursues what Buddha calls "right livelihood," that is, he raises the bread for the commune. I once was with a group of ex-convicts who had started a commune up in the mountains outside of Los Angeles. There were about a hundred of them and they would break into groups of eight and lie out in the woods with their heads touching and all take LSD with their wives and children. They had quite a powerful community and they were wondering what to do, because after a certain point of working inside you begin to feel the pull of service, the pull of sharing or serving. It's like a karmic predicament you're in; you can only collect so much before you have to hand it over, spread it out, and then you can go back inside. And so, they asked me what to do and I said why didn't they open a shop in Laguna Beach, which they did. It is now a fantastically successful shop where they make the crafts up in the hills and ship them in. That whole process is one of building these different parts of ourselves, and people rotate through these various scenes.

The fourth component is visiting other ways of achieving consciousness. For example, I've been working with the Benedictine monks at a monastery to start work on an exchange program with ashrams in India, with growth centers, with the Hasids, and with the Sufis. Another example, this evening is the last formal lecture or discussion that I am going to be giving in the United States on this round, in this incarnation, I hope. (That's only an attachment too, of course.) I'm about

5

to leave and I'm going back into training now because I'm a beginner. I realize I'm really like the water boy on the team so I'm cashing in the chips and going back into the jungle. However, the first thing I'm going to do is go to South America to a Sufi training program. The Sufis are the mystic wing of the Moslem religion. You know them, perhaps, as the whirling dervishes. That's only one aspect of them. Gurdjieff was trained in the Sufi tradition, primarily. After that, I'll go back to India. Now these are the kinds of things I'm talking about as the fourth stage. So, what I'm saying is that this evening is part of my work on myself because I realize that *the only thing you have to offer to another human being, ever, is your own state of being.* You can cop out only just so long, saying I've got all this fine coat—Joseph's coat of many colors—I know all this and I can do all this. But everything you do, whether you're cooking food or doing therapy or being a student or being a lover, *you are only doing your own being, you're only manifesting how evolved a consciousness you are.* That's what you're doing with another human being. That's the only dance there is! When you're protesting against somebody, the degree of consciousness with which you're protesting determines how well they can hear what it is you're really saying.

Consciousness as Freedom from Attachment

Consciousness does not mean attachment to polarity, at any level. It means freedom from attachment. And once you see that the highest mother is the mother who is the most *conscious* mother, the highest student, the highest therapist, the highest lover, the highest anything is the most conscious one, you begin to see that the way you serve another human being is by freeing him from the particular attachments he's stuck in that turn him off to life. You realize that the only thing you have to do for other human beings is to keep yourself really straight, and then do whatever it is you do.

I stop at a Shell station, and the man starts to wash my windshield and put in gas. I've got an old Buick usually, a 1938

6

limousine, and I live in it, and I'm driving around, and I'm sitting there with one leg under me, driving along at 45 miles an hour, full speed, and I'm doing my *mantra* . . . I'm doing my cognitive centering device. When I stop I'm in a very high state of consciousness just from doing that. I haven't been going anywhere, the car's doing it. It's like a movie of driving down the road in an old Buick. It's like cinerama, a four-day movie of cinerama. I'm just sitting. I've got a really good seat, and I see it all. I stop at the Shell station and I look at the man and of course he is somebody Central Casting sent over—right?—to give me gas and wash my windshield. He is playing like he's a Shell service man. He and I are both from Central Casting. I've been billed this round, in his consciousness, as a kind of strange far-out-looking guy in a weird old car and he is billed as a Shell salesman in my karmic unfolding. We meet, right there. At the moment he's washing my windshield and I look at him and . . . it's saying, "How's the show going, man?" He says, "Groovy." But you don't say it quite that way, you just . . . be there. Nothing to do, you don't come on to anybody, you don't have to change anybody. Just look at them. And so, he finishes and he starts talking about old cars, and then about how during this meat strike he carried turkeys in a car just like this back in 1929, or '39, rather, into New York City and sold them down the market. After we've been going at this for a while and I'm just signing my credit card slip he says, "Would you like to see my car?" "O.K." I get out and go see his car. It's a Mercedes and we look at that and talk about Mercedes. He says, "Say, I'd really like to have you meet my wife." "O.K." So we go upstairs—his wife lives upstairs—and we sit down with his wife. She says, "Would you like to stay for lunch?" "Sure."

So I stay for lunch and pretty soon his son comes home from college and we're all settling in, and we've all got our feet up and we're all home. I realize, this is my home. Where am I? Am I going to say, "Well, I gotta go home?" How did I define what that concept is all about? Here I am and here we are. We're here again, we're all here. Behind the Shell man and behind the weirdo, here we are! I begin to see that every moment of my life is that same place. So, tomorrow when I get in a car and go from Topeka to Albuquerque, the question is how much of my consciousness is spent going to Albuquerque, how much consciousness is spent leaving Topeka, and how much consciousness is right here and now, wherever here and now happens to be on the highway. To the extent that I keep the mantra going all the time, I will stay right here all the time. I can never get more than a little flicker away and I'm pulled right back to the here and now. So from the Shell man I begin to see that *the environment is as high as I am.* If I come to the station thinking I'm just a guy getting gas, that's all I am—a guy getting gas. The Shell man goes through his platitudes and I go through mine and I drive away. And that's what my whole life becomes. My whole life becomes this exquisite dance of being in one role after another where we do our on-stage routine, we do our *Lady Macbeth* scene again or *Twelfth Night* or *Blithe Spirit* or whatever it is we're doing.

Higher Consciousness as a State of Unity

It's easy to know this when you're sitting up in a cave. It's quite easy to sit and meditate and realize how all this is, to see how you get stuck in roles and how the life process, the spiritual contact, turns off the minute you think you're somebody doing something. As long as I think I am speaking to you and I'm doing something to you—forget it!—I'm just keeping you out there as "them." The question is, are you *them* or are you *us*? If I think of you using any model in my head that keeps you being *them*, I end up turning off myself. My consciousness, my concepts of the universe have turned me off because I know that the higher consciousness state is a state of unity. It is, "Here we are." I have experienced that. I know that. That's valid. It's absolutely obvious, now, that every time I perform an act which increases the distance, that kind of subject-object distance, I am taking myself one little

8

jot further away from that unitive state which I now know, *is*. Only an idiot is going to bring himself down. . . .

MANTRA

A mantra is a phrase, or it could be a sound or a phrase. It is a phrase that you repeat over and over and over again. Take for example the phrase, the Tibetan one (you can use English ones, but . . . I'll show you why you use Sanskrit or Tibetan ones) *Om Mani Padme Hum*. This phrase is perhaps one of the most widely used mantras in the world today. In fact in Nepal you'll see rocks twenty feet long and ten feet high with *Om Mani Padme Hum* written in tiny letters over the whole rock, so you can just read it like a letter. And there are prayer wheels at the temples where written in them ten million times is the phrase *Om Mani Padme Hum* . . . and you see lamas going around stupas saying *Om Mani Padme Hum*. Now, when you first start to say a mantra, the first involvement is in hearing it outside, through your ears, saying it aloud and hearing it and thinking about its meaning. That's the first game you play with mantra. So, if I give you that mantra, *Om Mani Padme Hum*, you think about it and you think, "Well, what does it mean?" Now, there are many meanings—there's a whole book written about its meaning by Lama Govinda. One of the ways of understanding its meaning is that *Om* means, like Brahma, that which is behind it all, the unmanifest. *Mani* means jewel or crystal. *Padme* means lotus, and *Hum* means heart. So, on one level what it means is the entire universe is just like a pure jewel or crystal right in the heart or center of the lotus flower, which is me, and it is manifest, it comes forth in light, in manifest light, in my own heart. That's one way of interpreting it. You start to say *Om Mani Padme Hum* and you're thinking, "God in unmanifest form is like a jewel in the middle of a lotus, manifest in my heart." You go through that and feel it in your heart—that's one trip. O.K., that's the first. That's the lowest level of operation of mantra. It's putting one set of thoughts into your head in place of another set of thoughts. Instead of thinking, "Gee, it's hot out. Shall I have a milk shake at the next stop? Gee, the engine sounds a little strange. Those new Chevy's don't look very good at all. Boy, I've been on this trip!" Instead of all of that stuff, which is terribly profound and important, but isn't really that relevant, you go into the mantra.

Once the mantra has been going on that way for a while, it starts to change in its nature. You stop thinking about what it means; you just get sort of addicted or hooked on the Tibetan sound of it. And then it starts to move into your head, and then from your head sort of down into your chest, until pretty soon it's going around like a little wheel, going around inside your chest, just *Om Mani Padme Hum*. Right? Now, at that point it has stopped meaning anything to you. Any time you want to bring it back into consciousness, you can rerun its meaning, which will do that thing for you again. But you can keep it down in the place where it's just running off. Now, it's got another quality to it. That is, when a mantra is done sufficiently it gets into a certain kind of vibration or harmony with the universe in a certain way which is its own thing. The conscious beings who evolve certain languages such as Sanskrit specifically evolve the sounds of these languages to be connected with various states of consciousness—unlike the English language—so that a Sanskrit mantra, if you do it over and over again, will take you to a certain state of consciousness.

The Mandala Process

In Tibet, for example, they use what are called *tonkas*. If you go to a doctor in Tibet, instead of giving you a prescription like, "Pick these herbs by a damp rock" or "Go to your local pharmacy and get. . . ." Instead of doing that, he often may give you a tonka, a mandala, to take home and put up on your wall and meditate upon. Now this is really far out, you see, because here's your doctor, you go to him because you've got headaches, or because you're depressed, or because you've got fear, or because you've got bleeding or something, and he gives you a piece of paper to stick up on your wall and meditate on. Now you'd say, "Well, that's pretty primitive." But wait a moment, just assume, for example, that they're not all nuts, see, and they're not all naive. And you go and sort of sit down in front of this paper and figure out what it's about. After a while you learn that the way these are designed is such that you put your focal attention on the entire mandala, which is a circle within a square and the square has gates, four gates. And then pretty soon your attention—you just let yourself be with that thing, let all other thoughts go and just stay with it— pretty soon, your attention is drawn in through the gates and in and in to the inner circle and into the innermost circle where there is a specific design or being or something and when you come in and in and in, you then experience the inner circle as something like a long tube. It takes on a depth, and as you stay with that inner circle you get drawn, literally drawn, your awareness gets drawn through that tube, and you get drawn from that tube into, literally, another frequency of vibration.

It is as though that model in the center of that little circle changes your consciousness because you have brought your consciousness down to just that circle. It's like, if you go into the Fillmore Auditorium and there are huge rock and roll bands and twenty-five slide projectors and an overloading of the stimulus field, that will take your consciousness into another place. Now, you can struggle against it, and say, "Oh, I'm getting a headache and I've got to get out of here. I mean, they're not feeding me linear information." Or you can say, "Well, here goes," and just sort of surrender into this and then there is a new level of consciousness where you are experiencing all these things . . . in a Gestalt form, rather than in linear separate components. You've given up one type of analytic thought because it's not adaptive at that moment.

Well, a mandala, very much like what's called faith healing, is based on the idea that "mind manifests in matter" and that if you change the nature of the vibrations or the nature

11

of the level of consciousness, you'll find certain levels of consciousness where certain illnesses don't exist. What a faith healer does is use his own vibrational rate to bring you to another vibrational rate. That's the way that process works. These tonkas work the same way. Well, a mantra works the same way. That is, it'll take you to its place. Now there are mantras that are very strong power mantras. There are mantras for every particular thing you could want, but the only kinds of mantras that are primarily used in the West, and the ones that I work with, are all what are called general mantras. Wherever you are, they'll take you further on. It's sort of an infinite progression. It's not committed to any level other than the final level, which is no level. *Om Mani Padme Hum* is one of them. After you've been doing it for awhile it starts to affect your consciousness. It's just like when you do *pranayama*, breath control. After you've been doing the basic breathing exercises for just a few months, your breath gets very gentle and even, and instead of the gross breath environment most of us live in, if you watch a yogi's breath it's always just very faint, a very delicate breath. That breath is the environment in which your consciousness is living all the time. It's a very intimate environment that most of us don't notice at all because we're just so used to whatever our breath is. We think that's the way it is. But when we start to create that calm breath, it starts to bring us into another space.

Now in addition to that, it serves as what would be called a centering device. That is, here is your predicament: you are stuck most of the time, just as I am, in the "illusion." That is, you are attached to something in time and space. You are identifying with your body, your feelings, with your thoughts, with your feet, you know. And the idea of a mantra is that it just sits there, and all that stuff goes by. It's like a bridge on which you stand, looking down into the water in which you see your own life going by. It's a training device to break you out of your attachments. When I'm driving and doing mantra I'm not attached to my driving. I'm doing mantra, and driving is just happening. So, in other words, the mantra is a technique for bringing me into a place in myself which would be called the eternal present; that is, a place where nothing is literally happening at all. It's a device for calming my mind.

THE ETERNAL PRESENT

Mantra gets so far out, that after I did it for two days and two nights solid in Nepal once, I stopped to go to sleep and of course it continued going. But instead of it continuing going just in *my* voice it continued going . . . what it sounded like was a cross between the Mormon Tabernacle Choir and the O Heavenly Day Chorus. It's that huge a thing except it was made up of all old voices and they stretched back in time and space in infinite direction. All I heard was *Om Mani Padme Hum* and the wind was *Om Mani Padme Hum* and the air conditioner was *Om Mani . . .* , the whole thing. I had tuned in on that place where that was all I could hear. But it was no longer my voice. I went rushing to a yogi and I said, "What's happening? I'm going crazy." He said, "You've tuned in on the *Om*, that's that place. You've tuned in on that place. There it is. That's where they're all hanging out."

My teacher is so delicate; he's a very beautiful Brahman. He said to me, "Don't eat any food that isn't cooked with love or with mantra . . . because it will poison you. The vibrations of a person cooking food enter into the food when it is cooked over fire." Fire transmutes, converts, brings that energy. . . . Well, now I can go into a restaurant along the road and eat something that is cooked by an angry chef and I won't experience it because I am so gross yet. My teacher would get violently ill; but even if the food were brought to him by a loving person and he didn't know anything about who cooked it, he would still get ill, because those vibrations are as real, as you get nauseous from the color green or blue or purple or whatever your thing is. Now at another level he could take that energy and transmute it, because that's the whole issue of transmuting energy.

When I said that God came to the United States in the form of LSD, I was quoting my teacher, with whom I lived for six months, who was, as far as I could see, one of the purest and highest beings I have met. When I asked him what LSD was he went away and several weeks later he came back and he wrote, and the quote is almost exact, "LSD is like a Christ coming to America in the *Kali-Yuga*. America is a most materialistic country and they wanted their Avatar in the form of a material. The young people wanted their Avatar in the form of a material. And so they got LSD. If they had not tasted of such things, how will they know—how they will know?" was his actual wording. Now, this plus the fact that my guru took 900 micrograms of LSD and nothing happened to him, and I watched this process happen, were the two bits of new information I had collected about LSD which I reported back to the intellectual community. I am not at this moment using LSD nor am I not using LSD. Right, I'm doing a type of yoga which does not require at this moment the use of LSD.

I honor LSD; LSD has, for me, anyway, made a major change in my perceptual field, and I feel that under suitable conditions it is a major breakthrough of technology, allowing man to change his levels of consciousness. I share Tim's vision in almost every way. I think I'm not as attached to certain kinds of polarities in terms of establishment and good and evil and dropping out and so on as Timothy is, but I think he is a great visionary and my feelings about LSD are: I honor it. I also think that it is very quickly becoming an anachronism. I think it is totally falling out of date because the types of consciousness that it opened allowed the Maharishi to do the work he did in the United States and allowed the Beatles to do the work they've done and allowed all of that process to happen. I think that only took about five years and it seems to me that the values in the culture shifted dramatically enough, as a result of the psychedelic movement, to bring in another set of cognitive consciousness possibilities into the *Zeitgeist*, enough so that they would become researchable, they would become studyable, and explorable; and yoga, which was a dirty word seven years ago, can now become a highly respected and thoughtful science, as it should be, as it is.

It is an entirely different matter for people who have known of an experience of another state of consciousness to work on themselves than for people who have not. If I observe the Gurdjieff students, a lot of students, those that come into a group in order to get some kind of group affiliation and are just good, pure people, can meditate and do the work for long times and very little happens. However, as my teacher said, "If a person knows of such things, then. . . ." And that's mainly what all of the Indian literature says—that once you know, once you have tasted of this possibility, then your work becomes tremendously directed toward this . . . then your meditations work at a much, much faster rate. So that, in terms of the statistics with the Maharishi Mahesh group, of the numbers of drop-outs from the program, it is clear that a large percentage of people originally were not able to maintain that degree of involvement because they didn't have a frame of reference which made them able to use the mantra in the spirit in which it was invested. There is no doubt that the Maharishi teaches a classical method that works beautifully. It is just what he says it is. It does just what he says it does. And when the investment is made in the spirit and received in the spirit, it has done remarkable things to thousands of people. If you come into it as an experiment to see if it will work, or come into it for a lot of other reasons, there is a very, very high probability you will drop out unless you're really ready, unless you're ready—let's put it that way.

I did a *Playboy* interview four years ago, before I went to India. See, that was a phony panel. It was put together by the editors of *Playboy* to make a colorful article and we were all asked a series of questions and I had answered those questions four years ago before I had ever done any yoga. Then when they sent it to me now, they said, "You've already sold us this article. We have the right to use it. We're going to use it. Are there any changes you want to make? You have only a day to make them and they should be minimal." So all I did was add the new information that I had which was: (*a*) what my guru did, (*b*) what my teacher did, and (*c*) the fact that I am not now using LSD. Those all went into the article. And those clues were the clues that I had to contribute to my fellow man at this moment.

THE "BOOK"

The book came about in a very strange way. I was in the temple in India and I was with my guru and a lot of remarkable things had been happening to me there and I kept some notes in a little book. One day the teacher came to me and he said, "Maharaji," meaning my guru, "sent his blessings for your book." So I said, "Well, what book is that?" and he wrote "Whatever book it is you're doing." So I thought, "Well, obviously I'm supposed to do a book," because you don't get any better instructions than that, in that scene. They don't say, "Now go out and . . . ," you know, "Do that, team." It's not that way. You just do whatever it is you're supposed to do. So I figured I'm supposed to do a book. So I came home and as any good intellectual academe, I sat down and I typed a book, *My Journey to the East: Fantastic Adventures*, that kind of thing. And I sent it to all these publishers and they all sent it back, and they said, "Well, our fall line of interesting mystical journeys to the East is full for this year and maybe you can try another publisher." And I thought, "Well, obviously that isn't the book, because, I mean, *he* knows what he's doing. He's not going to give me a blessing for a book he doesn't want to happen and if he's turning it down, he's obviously the publisher too." So I thought, that isn't the book. So I let it sort of hang for a year or so. And then people started to gather and I started to do this talking for a couple of years, at no charge, because I was no book, I was just doing it when people would drop by. I was going to sit in my cabin for a whole year and then go back to India. That was my original plan, since nobody told me I was supposed to do anything. And I realized that any game I do comes out of my own ego. My job was just to work on myself, and if anything happens, it happens.

Well, my impurity became very apparent to me. It was an exquisite impurity, the way all this happened. I was living in this little town of Franklin, and I went to the grocery store. My father was up for the weekend, and he said to me, "Take my new Cadillac." So I got into his new Cadillac, which of course blew my mind, you know, *Sadhu* renunciate driving a new Cadillac. I thought, "The boys in India should see me now!" And I am driving into town and I see two hippies over on the side of the road, a couple, and I wave at them and they at me. I go into the grocery store and I come out and there are five or six of them standing there. One of them comes over to me and he says, "Hey, man, you got any acid?" And I thought, "Oh-oh, I've been found out, who I'm supposed to be, you know; my history's caught up with me . . . my karma, I can't change, you know. They see I'm Richard Alpert, notorious drug man." So I said, "No, why do you ask?" They said, "Well, we heard a connection was coming up from Boston today and we saw this big Cadillac with masked plates and this guy with a beard and we figured you must be him." So I said, "Well" . . . see now, here is my impurity, the next line is the statement of my own impurity. All I had to say at that point was, "Well, I'm not him. See ya," and get in the car and drive back into my woods. But, the other line I used—which was my own desires, which is why we're here tonight—is the line, "Gee, I'm sorry, I'm not *that* kind of connection." That's a leading line like, "Come on, baby, don't you want to know what kind of connection I am? I sure look interesting, don't I?" So, of course, I'm asked, "Well, what kind of a connection are you?" and so on, and that leads to them dropping by and then them bringing up their friends, and their friends bring the parents, and the parents bring the minister, and the newspapers, and then the universities.

Wherever I was asked, I went. So it was the Rotary Club and Borscht Belt hotels and universities and hippie hangouts and communes. And I shared whatever I was supposed to do. So all of these started to be taped. It's a big generation of collecting stuff, so people would collect tapes. And then this groovy woman, you know, typed them all up, till it was a stack, a huge stack of these tapes from everywhere. Then this writer, John Bleibtreu, on the West Coast, was reading through them, and he said, "You know, there's really two beings in these tapes. When you start out one of these tapes usually you're being very professory, you're talking heavy, you're teaching but when the audience is a certain way and they let it happen to you, it's as if you disappear and something starts to happen so all the words come out sort of like in iambic pentameter. They're not like you're talking at all, it's just like there's beautiful stuff coming out, except it's all 1970ish stuff. It's a lot like the *Book of Tao*, but it's sort of '70ish." So we said, "Well, why don't we cut out all the heavy parts and we'll put that together." Since I didn't say it, you see it isn't me saying it, maybe this is his book. He's writing his own book. He doesn't trust me, he doesn't want my heavy mind writing his book, he's going to write his own book. So we started to put all this stuff together, and we got a book. There's a group in New Mexico and, as I said last night, they start with these four-foot pieces of cardboard and this book is 108 pages and each day they meditate from five to eight in the morning—there's a group of five of them—and then all in silence . . . they hand rubber-stamp each page, all the letters of the page, and then the artists do all the sketching around the thing. Then the whole thing is photo-reduced and shipped to Japan where it's printed on rice paper and hand stitched because it's an experiential-type document. So that was the basis of the book and I was going to do 20,000 of those and split. That was my deal with Maharaji.

And then people said, "Well, if you're going to do it would

you include that long bibliography on mysticism that you've been working on?" So, "O.K. I'll put that in." Then somebody else said, "You've got all these quotes you read all the time from Buddha and so on. Would you put those in, like little cards we can hang up, cards you can put up on the screen door as you're going out—'The journey of a thousand miles begins with a single step,' by Chuang Tsu. And you've got one for over the toilet and one for going to bed and one for over the refrigerator." So we thought we'd put in a deck of those. Then somebody said, "You know, you've got all these pictures of these high beings and you hang out with them. Why can't we hang out with them? Could you put a set of them, put in two sets so if we take them out we won't ruin the book." "O.K. We'll put those in too." And then somebody else said, "Say, you know that long fancy book, my parents aren't going to understand it, you know. Could you do something very straight, like for my parole officer or my parents or whoever . . . ?" "O.K., we'll do a nice straight journey-to-India type story. Just tell the facts of the whole matter and . . ." So we put that in. And then somebody else said, "You know, you've been talking about diets and about *asanas* and about breathing and you've been teaching this stuff about how to live and how to . . . what kind of world you start to create to change consciousness. Couldn't you put in sort of like a cookbook-type thing for people who say, 'All right, I want to do it, now what do I do?' for doers?" So we've got a psychic cookbook in there, too. A do-it-yourself enlightenment kit. And then people said, "You know, you chant, and I've been chanting with this girl and she plays the dulcimer and I play the tamboura and we just go out together on these far-out chants, Indian chants. Could you put in one of those throw-away records like *Look* or *Life* puts out, those little cheap records?" Well, that turned into a twelve-inch record on both sides. So that's in there. So it became a box instead of a book. And the box had a big mandala on the front of it, and the box is called *From Bindu to Ogis*. Bindu is sexual energy and Ogis is spiritual energy, and it's the transformation of energy within the body through the conversion of a form of energy. It's called the raising of the *Kundalini*, is one way of talking about it.

So, 20,000 of those are being made and they're all going to be given away. Your paying to come here gets you one, because you've already paid for it, since the money from this is green energy which goes to buy that. And then when you get the book, I'm done. It all comes out even in the end, right? When it's ready we'll write to you and say, "Your book's ready, do you want it?" and then I've fulfilled my karmic responsibilities as far as I'm concerned. The book is authorless. I mean there are about fifty of us working on it and there are no names connected with it. It's just Maharaji's book, I guess. It's not copyrighted.

PSYCHOTHERAPY AS A PATH

Psychotherapy is just as high as the psychotherapist. If your psychotherapist happened to be Buddha, you would get enlightened in the process, see. I'm not being facetious, now, but I'm saying that when you cut aside all the melodrama, you will get as free of your particular role-attachments as the psychiatrist is free of his. Because if he is still attached to his particular role, all he can do is give you one role to substitute for another, which is primarily his. So that generally Freudian patients end up Freudianized and Jungians end up Jungianized. Now most therapists have a model of what they think they're doing and how it all works, so any data that's fed in from the patient goes through this model and out comes a response consistent with this model.

For eight years I was a psychotherapist, among other things, at the Harvard Health Service and the Stanford Health Service and Cal and so on, and I would spend a day a week. I had eight patients and I would sit there and I would run them through my Freudian theories. After I had taken psychedelics for a while I began to see that the model I was using was standing in the way of real change at times, because since I was busy being a doctor at some level or other since that was the only role available to me—doctors needed patients, that's the symbiotic thing that you do, that's who you hang out with—so there's only room for one of us being the doctor, and I'm it. I may have as many hangups as you have but we've decided the game is that I'm the doctor this time and therefore you're the patient. And the question is how a patient ends being a patient. It's like, "Psychoanalysis Terminable or Interminable" —another level of understanding that article by Freud. So I thought, "Well, as long as I'm busy being a doctor, I need patients, and every time a person stops acting like a patient, I have to get rid of him, because he's not fulfilling whatever it is I need."

GAME THEORY

I was teaching game theory at that time as a psychodynamic device, not as a joke but as a way of . . . I was teaching it in junior high schools actually. I was teaching a mental hygiene course, teaching kids how to do behavior change in themselves through game-analysis of their own game roles and so on. They were very hip, those kids. They'd say, "Is there a non-game center?" And I'd say, "No, no, no," or "I don't know," or "Don't worry about that," or "You're not ready," see, because I didn't know what to answer at that time. So I changed my therapy deal, which seemed like a kind of external "hype," but it was symbolic of something a little deeper. I started to have the person sit next to me and we had a big chalk board up there and we would chart his game. He brought the data and I brought the research theories. He was my research collaborator in this behavior-change problem. And what I did was, I was immediately setting up a dissociative thing with the "patient" so that the part of him that was sick was the part that *we* were studying and the relationship I was having with him was as a researcher of his own sickness. That is, I was immediately separating him from his sickness by saying, "The guy who you and I are relating to isn't the sick guy, O.K.?" Now that was phony, and it was real. It was a little of each. Then I went to India and I started to get into other kinds of spaces and understandings and I came back and I realized that to the extent that I didn't think at all, didn't get stuck in any role, I was going to be the optimum use to him.

I've got to feed in one experience that I had that seems relevant. I was in England and I was with a psychiatrist by the name of Ronnie Laing. Ronnie and I decided to take LSD together. And he said to me, "How much shall we take?" I said, "Well, why don't we take about 300 micrograms?" And he said, "Well, that's a little much for me. But as long as you're along, I guess it's all right." Now by his saying that he put me into the role of sort of being his protector, that is, he cast me into the role of being the guide, which bugged me a little bit. But O.K. I don't know this guy. If that's the trip I'm supposed to play, I will be John Responsible. And he can flip around the room, right? And my usual model of what's going to happen is I'm going to take it and I'm going to create a pleasant environment. I'm going to put on Miles Davis records (in those days) and we're going to lie around and, you know, do it. So we take this and the first thing that happens after we've taken these chemicals is he takes off all his clothes but his shorts and he starts to stand on his head. This doesn't fit into my model of what you do when you have psychedelics. I don't know anything about yoga, and it all seems absurd to me. This is five, six, seven years ago. So I watch with a certain, you know, disbelief. Then he walks over to me and he looks into my eyes and his face looks like the most defenseless child, just like my model had been that I'm going to have to take care of him . . . I'm going to be the guide. He looks like a totally defenseless child. He arouses in me every nurturant impulse I have. I feel tremendously protective of him. And I just feel like saying, "Oh, Ronnie . . . ," I'm not saying anything but I'm like, "Ronnie, it's all right, I'm here." You know, "Count on me." He's just like a little child, wide open. And we were no sooner in that role than his face takes on the subtlest change, just muscle patterns like, it's as if a thought in his head manifests in a change in his face—he now looks like the most protective, fatherly, warm, nurturant being—and he arouses in me all those uncooked seeds of being a little, dependent child, see. And I become, "Oh, Ronnie, oh, wow, you will take care . . . You are going to be my . . . Oh, Ronnie, I can do it this time. Oh, Wow." The minute I'm in that, his face changes again, and he is now the student and he's asking me questions. This is all silent. It's all mime and all just facial things. It's all thought forms.

I had once taken LSD in New York City. I was going to the David Susskind Show, I think, and I put my consciousness in the right place. I took this and I had several hours before I had to go to the studio and I was at an uptown penthouse-type thing. There was a girl there drawing people's faces on the walls with crayon. I mean the apartment owner wanted her to make a set of faces along the stairway wall. So she asked me if I would pose, and I said I'd be delighted. My mind was in liquid form and I stood there and I thought, "Well, who is it I am? Who is it she's drawing?" I thought, "She's drawing a young man looking into the future." So I became like, well . . . it's like you see the sun just . . . the sunrise is just over there and you're just . . . that feeling of . . . you've seen so many pictures like that. They're always life insurance. And I'm *just* looking into the future and she starts to draw me. She's very sure of herself and the lines are all very fierce. And then I'm sort of bored with looking into the future. I know I can't change my face, because that would ruin her picture, so I just start to think I'm somebody else. Now I think I'm her lover. I don't do anything, I just think I'm her lover. After about thirty seconds she erases and erases and erases. She's got to draw this thing in a new way. And after a while I think, "Well, I don't think I'm going to make it as her lover. That doesn't feel quite right," you know. Then I thought, "Really I'm an old, wise man." And she erased again and started to draw.

Finally she said, "I can't do your face; it's just like plastic. It keeps changing." Well, Ronnie and I in the course of the next six hours went through, I don't know, perhaps eighty or so different social roles. What we did was we'd go into a role, a symbiosis, like therapist and patient, and then we'd flip it around and be patient and therapist. We'd be executioner and prisoner and then prisoner and executioner. Some of them really scared us, believe me. It really is scary. In each one you had to say, "Right, O.K., that one," and then flip over and do the reverse of it. And I began to see that Ronnie and I were establishing a contact in the place where we were behind all of that. You could say behind the people that were playing the game. It's like in an English tennis match at the set point when they're fighting for this point and they look up at each other and say, "Jolly good game." "Yes, jolly good." And then they're back into the game. You see, it's that up-level of, "Here we are and the sun's out and it's really beautiful, isn't it?" And the most powerful statement of that I've ever heard connected with LSD was in the *World Medical News*, the work of Eric Kast giving LSD to terminal cancer patients. One cancer patient had said, "Yes, I know I'm dying of the deadly disease but look at the beauty of the universe." That is, she was able through that experience, or in the midst of that experience when LSD was properly administered under the right conditions, to see the process of dying as a process of dying and still identify free of "she who is dying." Then the fear disappears. Most of the difficulty you have in the dying process is the fear connected with death. In fact, many difficulties on many planes are connected with that, many planes.

GUIDE OF CONSCIOUSNESS JOURNEYS

So when I come back from India now and after that experience with Ronnie, I'm not doing anything and people come to see me and they are hung up in some way. Now I'm a yogi, see. But after all, I'm trained as a psychotherapist, so I'm still a psychotherapist. And I've been guiding the psychedelic ses-

sions so I'm still in some sense a guide of consciousness journeys, even though I'm not working with drugs any more. All
that stuff instead of being lost just seems to be amalgamating.
It's summating in some way. So now I'm doing an interesting
thing. I look into somebody's eyes (I may look into their eyes
anywhere from thirty seconds to ten hours) but when I look
into their eyes, I'm not really looking into their eyes. That's the
first thing. I'm looking at a point right between their eyes.
Slightly above, right here. And as a result of focusing on that
point, I am able to see both eyes, first thing. The second thing
is, I'm sitting there doing *Om Mani Padme Hum*. In other
words, I empty my mind completely. So that I am merely, if
you will, a mirror, since I have no game going. There's nothing;
all I'm doing is bringing myself to my center and focusing, just
as if I were focusing on a candle flame. It is not interpersonal,
in any sense. I'm not saying, "Are you there? I am here. Hello.
I love you. Don't worry, you can trust me." None of that. It's
just, you know, candle flame, it's one-pointedness. Now I have
finally, after this work of the past year, defined a little game
which is called Guts Ball, see. When I was in the temple in
India, whatever I thought, it turned out the guru knew. And as
I told you last night, even the most horrible, innermost, intimate, frightening, scary thoughts, even the ones that after five
years of analysis, $30,000 later, I still hadn't fully in their full
flavor shared with the analyst—not because I didn't want to,
but because the flavor was so rich I could never find the way
to share those particularly perverse fantasies, or whatever they
were. More like a posturing than a total. I mean you can tell
them the gross thing, you can say anything you want in an abstract enough way and it has no effect. It's when you get into
the flavorings and the colorings that you get the affective components. I say to the person, "When I was with my guru, I
realized that he knew it all from inside. He looked at me and
he saw that place in me where I was behind all that, so he
didn't get hooked on 'I am a neurotic' or 'I am a bad person' or
'I am a good person' or 'I am anything.' He just saw me almost

25

as life and he could feel the merging of love and light with that being inside me, behind all that." And I say, "Just like the Sikhs, a religious order in India, say, 'Once you realize God knows everything, you're free.' That is, once you realize that it's all right (the whole model of original sin, in other words), once you've seen that you're not the original sinner, you are free."

Now when my guru did this to me and when I suddenly realized there was another human being so deeply inside my own head that we were both looking at it from the same place, and with all that, here he was totally accepting, I experienced this tremendous sense of freedom and exhilaration and well-being. And it changed my behavior because then I found the truth was no longer too expensive, truth was now an absolute prerequisite in the dance, because if I wanted to be high with everybody all I had to do was let them in. I didn't have to go around letting people in like the ancient mariner with the albatross around his neck, telling the story in a preoccupied way, but I had to be able to let another person in. The guru was already in and it was all right, so it was obviously all right.

SIMPLE RULE OF THE GAME

So now what I say to the person is, "That's one of the things that he did for me. Maybe I can do that for you. So the simple rule of this game is that you like to play. I'll explain the rules of the game but you'd better only play if you want to play because you can only play if you want to play anyway. Even if you make believe you want to play, that won't be good enough. So the rules of the game are this: anything you can think—and you might all try this on for size, it's kind of fun just to look inside—anything you can think, feel, desire, fear, anything you can bring to your mind about any of these, that you have difficulty with, are embarrassed by, are made uncomfortable by sharing with me—share it with me." It's a simple rule of the game. In other words, I'm saying to you, like in Hermann Hesse's magic theater, "Any door you've got closed, open. Let's get on with it. You and I are sharing this thing. We're going to get on. . . ." And I say, "I'm not my guru, I can't go into your head because I choose to go into your head. I can only go into your head if you invite me into your head, and you can only invite me into your head if there's no way in which I am 'him.' Every thought you have that you've got to keep from me, keeps me 'him.' And finally when there's nothing in your head that you can't share with me, then we're 'us.' That's like you've been out on a hard day and you go home and you put your feet up and you throw your wallet on the table and you relax and you're home and there's 'us.' And 'us' knows all the foibles, etc." Let me just finish this sequence. So a person looks at me and I say, "You only play if you want to play." "Oh, yeah, I want to play, I want to play." Now I'm sitting looking between their eyebrows doing *Om Mani Padme Hum*, *Om Mani Padme Hum*, *Om Mani Padme Hum* and they look at me and they say, "I want to stick my penis up your nose," that's for openers. So I sit there doing *Om Mani Padme Hum*, *Om Mani Padme Hum* and it's just as if he had opened his mouth and gone, "a blah, blah, blah, blah," right? In other words, I don't have a theory going.

When I was a Freudian, somebody would say, "I've been thinking about my mother's vagina," and I write down, "mother's vagina," you know, and pretty soon I've got the patient reinforced so that every time I pick up my pencil he gets a flash. He's winning my attention and love. Pretty soon he's talking about his mother's vagina fifteen minutes of the hour. And then I think, "Ah, we're getting someplace." But now—it is literally true—there is nothing he can say to me that makes any difference at all. I couldn't care less what he says.

Then, he looks and he looks away, you know, and I say, "You can look at me, it's all right. Here we are." I say, "Right. You want to do that and here we are." And I'm doing *Om Mani Padme Hum*, *Om Mani*. . . . He says, "Gee," and after that one he feels so good he says, "You look like Buddha,

there's light coming out of your head and you're so beautiful."
And inside me goes a little wave of, "Um-m-m, maybe I am,
maybe I am the Buddha." And inside goes *Om Mani Padme
Hum, Om Mani*. . . . And the *Om Mani Padme Hum* is
watching him say that, and me do my trip, and it's just watching it all. I'm just sitting there with my eyes on the light saying,
Om Mani Padme Hum, Om Mani Padme, just watching trans-
ference, countertransference, all of it, go under the bridge.
It's all just going . . . and I couldn't care less.

He says, "You know, your face just changed, you look
lecherous, evil; drool coming out of your mouth, and fire, and
I'm getting nauseous," and he's going through the whole thing
and I'm *Om Mani Padme Hum, Om Mani*. . . . Now what's
interesting is that I'm using this as a device for centering on
myself. I'm working on myself. That's all I can do. All I'm
doing is working on myself, which is my instruction always to
people who are therapists who ask me what do you do about
therapy. I say, "Work on yourself, see, because your 'patients'
will be as free as you are." That's why I come back to the
statement that therapy is as high as the therapist is. Now the
only other thing I would say in response to your question is
that each particular therapeutic school is related to one particular type of distribution of energy in the system, or *pran*.

CHAKRA CENTERS

If you think in terms of *chakras* or energy centers in the
body or connected with the body, there is the first, second,
third, fourth, fifth, sixth, and seventh, which are called the
muladhara, sradhishthana, manipura, anahata, vishuddha, ajna,
and *sahasrara*. The first one is at the bottom of the spine, the
second is sort of below the navel, the third is at the navel, the
fourth is in the heart region, the fifth is at the throat, the sixth
is between the eyebrows, the seventh is on the top of the head.
These don't necessarily have any physiological correlates.
They're just psychic localizations of psychic energy, let's put it
that way, in this Hindu system, a Sanskrit, Hindu system I

was talking about. Now, instead of doing an MMPI or a Rorschach you could also do a chakra chart, just like you could do an astrological chart. And these all tell you certain things. An astrological chart is like an MMPI one level back in abstraction. In the same way, a chakra chart tells, in a way, where the energy is fixed or localized in a person, where it's stuck.

For most people in the Western universe, in fact most people in the world, almost all of the energy is located either in the first, second, or third chakras. The first chakra can be characterized crudely as being connected with survival and survival of the individual as a separate being. It's like we're in the jungle and there's one piece of meat and who's going to get it, you or me? It's a survival-of-the-fittest-type model. It's a Darwinian assumption about the motivations of beings. When you're at that chakra, your motivation is to protect yourself as a separate being, your separateness. You can think of that as darkest Africa. And the channel up which this is all going is called the *Sushumna*—think of it as a big river. You go in the river from Africa and the next stop is like the Riviera. See, you've got your security under control and now you start to go into sensual gratification and sexual desires and reproduction. You can't be busy reproducing if you're protecting your life, but the minute your life's protected a little bit, then you can concern yourself with the next matter, which is reproducing the species. So the second chakra is primarily concerned with sexual actions, reactions, and so on—at the reproduction level. Procreative. Sex.

The third chakra is like Wall Street and Washington and London. It's primarily connected with power, with mastery, with ego control. Most of the world that we think of is connected with those particular centers. All the energy's located there. People justify their lives in terms of reproduction or sexual gratification, sensual gratification, or power or mastery. And it's interesting that pretty much any act we know of in the Western world can be done in the service of any one of those energies. So that a man can build a huge dynamic industry and we can say, "Aha, phallic," meaning second chakra. Or a person can seduce many women in order to have mastery and power over them and we say, "Aha, concerned with power and mastery," meaning third chakra. Doing sex in the service of third chakra.

Now it turns out—and this is the one that many of you will find hard sledding, but it's the way I understand it now, having been through this particular trip I've been through—that Freud is an absolutely unequaled spokesman and master of second-chakra preoccupation, that is, of those beings who were primarily involved in second chakra. So he could say quite honestly, because it is true at the second chakra, that religion is sublimated sex. Now it is true that in his generalized libido theories and the idea that all the body is erogenous. There are a lot of ways in which he slips over the edge; but his system is primarily concerned with the second chakra. Adler is primarily concerned with third chakra. Jung is primarily concerned with fourth chakra. I would point out that there are still the fifth, sixth and seventh chakras. And these are in terms of other kinds of psychic spaces and ways of organizing the universe and understanding what's happening. So that to the extent that you have "uncooked seeds" of the second chakra and you have a Freudian analyst, he's going to help you cook those seeds. He's not going to do much about where you're stuck in the third chakra, particularly. And he hasn't much to say about the fourth chakra, which is what Jung pointed out about Freud.

Now, you can take any of these theories and extend them out in many directions, but there is a discontinuous place between the third and fourth stage. There are many theories that are nonmystical and there are theories that are mystical. There are theories that deal with transcendent states and there are theories that don't. And when Jung starts to deal with his archetypes, collective unconscious and so on, he is starting to deal with what's called the fourth chakra, which is the same thing as Buddha's compassion. He is still in astral planes and he himself is afraid to go on. That's quite clear. He goes just so far and then he stops, because he's afraid that if he goes the next step, he will no longer be able to do what he does as Carl Jung. That's a very tricky place, to be able to surrender your game which you have certain mastery in, in order to go for more. But I'm afraid that everybody is driven to go for more until they can, in the depths of their inner being, say, "This is enough." And they can only say that when it is. So the press of evolution on man's consciousness is inevitable. There's nothing he can do about it. He doesn't really have much choice in the matter. He's just got to wake at the rate he's got to wake.

LEVELS OF CONSCIOUSNESS

Here is the predicament that one faces about this work. The goal of these efforts is a non-dualistic state. That is, the place you are reaching for is a state where there is only one. Not one versus anything else; just one. It all is. It's one. A non-dualistic state. To get to that place you use methods that are in dualism. Right? You use dualism to talk about it. You use dualism to go beyond dualism. All right. So that concerning all of the planes other than the plane of oneness, a Buddhist would say, "Don't get hung up in all that stuff because all you're doing is perpetuating dualism," right? A Mahayana Buddhist or another kind of Buddhist would say, "You can use dualism as a crutch to get yourself beyond dualism if you use it intelligently. You can use Guru Rimpoche or Padma-Sambhava, who is a being on another plane of reality, as a connection to work with, but you know that he's part of the illusion, too, and he's going to have to go finally. So if within that framework you can understand that anything I say about planes is all illusory and you and I both know that, then we can talk about planes. There's that level.

There are a variety of systems that project out a number of different planes. You can have three, seven, nine, and many more if you want to get into finer and finer gradations. I can only approach this matter of planes experientially through two places. One, I can do it through the variety of psychedelic

31

experiences that I've had where I have experienced various things which I kept in horizontal compartments in my head, sort of saying, "Well, that's that hallucination, and that's that one, and that's that one, and that's that one," sort of like in storage units waiting for retrieval when I'd have a model they'd fit into. And then along comes a model and I say, "Oh, that one is clearly 'blup,' " see, and that one's a "blup," and it all falls into place. And I say, "Aha, this system encompasses all the experiences I've had to date, anyway," all right? For example, at one point I take 900 micrograms of LSD standing in the ocean in the middle of the night in Mexico, right? Now I'm trying to get as close as I can to the primitive world, universe. I'm trying to work through my first chakra fears. So I'm standing there with the surf pouring around me and it's going to drag me out and I can feel the sand pulling out under my feet and I can feel the bugs biting me, which makes me want to dive into the surf, except that the stars and phosphorescence in the water have all become just jeweled carpet that surrounds me in a 360-degree sphere and I don't see which is up and down. I have a suspicion that if I go into that wave there's no way to come up out of it—since up and down seem to me to be the same thing at that point.

So I am there with that predicament and at that point it all turns into vectors. That is, all I see is fields of force. All I feel is energy forces and it's like I'm a point and there are these forces acting upon me, pushing me in one direction. It's all like a physics problem now. That's all that's left of the universe. At that point I see, most interestingly, that if I do go into the ocean then I die, but at the same moment I come into another harmony with the universe, and at either place I am in perfect harmony with the universe. So, now I have gone through an experience that one to me is life and death. I'm seeing that place. Then I'm saying, "Well, if one to me is life and death why am I staying alive?" And then I see that out of all these vectors, when I sort of summate them, like see where the force is, there is one added vector that is my link to my fellow human beings. It's like my incarnation as a member of this species is keeping me attached, so that I can't reject my species by killing myself. See, the act of dying is an act of suicide, which is an ego act. And I see that I must live on because I must live on, because that's the way the forces are acting. O.K. Now, I can find that level in many books describing the level where it is all gotten into a place of just patterns of energy. And I can say, "Well, now what I'm dealing with is a casual plane which is merely forces and counter forces." It's like the world of Yin and Yang, that level. There are times when I go into things where I start to meet other beings, which are like dreamlike beings or demons or whatever you want to call them. And I say, "Well, now I'm on certain other kinds of planes, as I see in the books."

The simplest system would say there is this physical plane, then within each of us there are three bodies. There is the physical, a subtle, and a causal body, if you want to call it that. The physical body is connected to your body and what you know yourself to be. The subtle body is connected to your personality, you emotions, your chakras, and so on, your thinking mind. Your causal body is the world of ideas out of which all that comes. It's like a pyramid and the ideas are the top place. They're like Plato's pure ideas. Behind that is a level where it's all homogeneous field. *The Tibetan Book of the Dead* deals with *bardos*, which is another statement of levels, coming back the other way. The seven chakras can all be connected with various planes of astral and causal place, this one being causal.

My general way of dealing with this is to ignore most of it. I mean I don't learn all of these systems because I'm not terribly interested. Because whatever it is that I see in "form," I've got to go beyond it, anyway, so why bother chronicling it? Once I understood that the job is to finish the journey in one lifetime, I'm just doing it. I'm just finishing the journey. So anybody I meet, any powers I gain, or anything, any beings that come along, I just say, "Groovy, baby. Cool it, 'cause I'm on my way." I'm like the rabbit in *Alice in Wonderland*. I can't stop, fellow, I'm sorry. I can't stop to groove in the heavens or be the God of the Wind or whatever the trip is. Those are all planes that we're dealing with. Now I know for some of you that's really far-out stuff. Sounds pretty nutty; and I haven't made a great effort to make that transition, to put it in psychodynamic terms and so on, because I feel that we are a very heterogeneous audience and some of us can hear it one way and some of us can hear it another; so I'm sharing my consciousness as well as I can.

KRISHNA

Jehovah has a very limited repertoire of emotional responses, as gods go. He can be righteous, he can be indignant, he can be punitive, he can be benevolent. That's about it. He's sort of like somebody's quite old grandfather. That's who Jehovah usually is. Now and then in one of the Psalms you get a little feeling that he could be a swinger, but not very much—it's just alluded to in the Bible. Usually he's very straight, you see. Well, in India the same being, whatever it is, is common property to all the religions of the world. They see the many forms of god and they see him in a variety of different roles.

For example, the farthest-out one for us Westerners perhaps is that of Krishna. There is a great religious story of Krishna sporting with the Gopis, the milkmaidens, on full moon nights by the river, where he plays his flute. He's about seventeen years old and he's handsome and a swinger, see. He plays his flute, and he plays it so beautifully that the chicks drop their milk pails and their babies and they leave their husbands and they leave the pots on the stove and they go flying to this guy, because when he plays his flute, that's it. He awakens that thing in them. And they rush to him—there are about 16,000 of them—and he manifests himself in 16,000 forms and he makes love to each of them just as they would most want to be made love to. They are making love with God, right? And then after their mad sport they all go into the river and bathe

34

and it's a wild scene, see. And this is as much like Passover or Yom Kippur or Rosh Hashanah or Good Friday; it's another one of the scenes, see, because in *Bhakti* Yoga—Yoga meaning union and Bhakti meaning the vehicle toward union using the heart chakra or devotion—there are eleven different ways in which you can be devoted to another being. You can be devoted to your father or like Mary to Jesus, like mother to child, or like a friend, like John and Jesus, or in this case like lover and beloved, which is certainly a very high human relationship. And the fact that you can use the relationship of lover and beloved to come into that oneness with God is a spiritual practice.

In fact, there is a sect in India who are worshipers of Krishna. They are Gopis. Now they're not transvestites though they dress as Gopis. They're men. They dress as milk maids and they are in the relation to Krishna of lover to beloved. All of these different relationships are possible. Now Ram is another of the incarnations of Vishnu, as is Krishna. In the Hindu system the one Brahma becomes the three: Brahma, Vishnu, Siva, meaning the Creator, the Preserver, and the Destroyer or Changer, to put it crudely. And Vishnu, the Preserver, has a number of incarnations, of which Krishna's one, and Ram is one, and Buddha's one, and so on. And Ram is a perfect statement of *Karma* Yoga. He's the perfect father, he's the perfect husband, he's the perfect lover, he's the perfect friend, he's the perfect servant, he's just a wonderful guy. He's a great king. The *Ramayana*, which is one of the holy books of India, concerns his story. Now like every great holy book, it's always written at a number of levels, and you read the level you're ready to hear. Like you can the Bible, the New Testament, as a teaching in higher consciousness when you're ready to read it that way, or you can read it as a melodramatic story of Jesus. There's the Jesus story and then there is Christ's consciousness. And you'll notice in the Bible there's always Christ sort of standing around saying, "Well, that's the way the prophecy said it. Well, tomorrow's the big day. Keep quiet, woman, it's not yet my time." I mean he's like directing the script. He knows how it all is.

And then there's Jesus carrying the cross and doing the thing and curing the people and doing his trip, saying, "Why are you going to sleep?" and stuff like that. "I told you to stay awake; why are you going to sleep?" That's the Jesus story, see. And then there's the Christ-consciousness. Well, in the same way in the *Ramayana*, and most of these other books, there are always these two levels.

RAM STORY

Example, at one point, Ram is going through the jungle and he meets these naked ascetics. And they say, "Hey, Ram, you're God and we're really being bugged by these demons; we can't meditate. Would you mind getting a mantra we could say that would get rid of them, cause they're making a lot of noise? You know, it's like cats making love on the back fence. They're really screwing up my meditation. Could you get me a mantra that would get rid of the blue jay so it wouldn't scare away all the other birds?" Ram says, "Well, I have to go see my guru," because he's a young man. So he goes many miles and he goes to see his guru; takes his wife with him, and his brother. He sees his guru and the guru is sitting in a house and takes one look and sees God coming toward him. So the guru runs out and falls on his face before Ram. Ram looks and sees his guru, so he runs and falls on his face before the guru. They're both down there honoring each other. Ram says to the guru, "I've come to get a mantra to help these ascetics." And the guru says, "Come on, baby, what do you mean? I mean, you're God. If you're God, you're the mantra and you're the demons and you're the whole business; so if you're all that, what do you need me for?" And then right in the middle of the sentence . . . "Oh, I forgot. We're in an incarnation and this incarnation you're a nice young man and I'm your guru, so of course I'll give you the mantra and I'll . . ." He gives him the mantra and he goes home and does his thing.

Now those are what I mean by the two levels at which these high books are written. At one point Ram's wife is taken away

36

by the bad man, Ravina, who is really a good man finishing up a bad incarnation, if you want to know the real plot. And Ram, of course, is beside himself, because his wife's been taken away, you know. She's pining away and she won't make it with the bad guy and she's going to die. He's determined to find her. He goes to the king of the monkeys and he asks for help. The king of the monkeys assigns his monkey lieutenant, Hanuman, to serve Ram. Hanuman becomes the perfect servant. Hanuman is a representative of pure, unadulterated service. He's not serving in order to take over Ram's job. He's not serving in order to get patted on the head by Ram. He's just serving because he serves. And Ram says to him, "Hey, Hanuman, who are you, man, monkey? And Hanuman says, "When I don't know who I am, I serve you. When I know who I am, you and I are one." So that's who Hanuman is. It turns out that the temple I was brought to is a Hanuman temple in India. They worship Hanuman. They are in the relation of devotee to God, in the relation of servant to master.

So my name is Ram Dass. Dass means "servant" and Ram is the name of that incarnation, so it means "servant of God." So my gig is to serve; so I am doing my service. As I say, when I know who I am, you and I are one, when I don't know who I am, I'm serving you. That's why I ask often, "How may I serve you?" because it's not like the movie "The Servant" where you're trying to take over power. It's where you're playing out your part in the drama by being a servant, it's just a pure relationship.

The Issue of Social Responsibility

It seems to me to be responsibility to the well-being of one's fellow man, and just as I said earlier, if you watch the way it often works, people can get locked in a struggle and then some other model can come which frees both of them from an untenable predicament that they're stuck in, right? In other words, somebody comes in with a new way of looking at it—like with two children fighting, you often can come in and get their

37

minds somewhere else so that the whole fight changes its nature and what they're fighting about doesn't seem to be the essence of the matter. It seems to me that the tensions in society today are much more profound than any specific external condition. Those are all manifestations of it, but it is itself not the war in Vietnam or not poverty. Einstein said an interesting thing, he said, "The world that we have made as a result of the level of thinking we have done thus far creates problems that we cannot solve at the same level as the level we created them at." That is, the only way we can solve them is by creating a new level of thinking about them. In other words, we've got to break the set.

When there is a kind of confrontation the confrontation usually increases the amount of hurt and anger and polarization, ultimately. That no matter what the short-term gain is, there is a long-term loss in terms of increasing paranoia. So that, especially in California, you can see the increasing polarization most, most dramatically. In high-energy centers in the country that polarization and paranoia seem to precipitate out much faster. If I identify with any side of any position, then my attachment to that side makes me see the opposite side in terms of an object, as "them." Seeing another being as "them" is what the problem is, that's what it boils down to. That is, whether it's nationalism or racial tension or generations or theories of research or whatever it is. To the extent that you see somebody in the universe as "them" you create increasing paranoia because you're stuck in your world of "them," which puts "them" in the world of "them" which increases the "themness," or subject-object, or psychic distance between people. So that, as I said earlier, I see that the only law or rule of all human relations, be they mother and child or therapist and patient or lecturer and audience or army and pacifist or North Vietnamese and South Vietnamese or whatever it is, the only rule of the game is to put your own consciousness in a place where you are no longer attached to a polarized position even

38

though you may by the nature of the game contracts you're involved in be forced to play out a polarized role.

For example, I recently met with this police chief who has been going around to colleges getting college students to become policemen for New York City. I complimented him on what he's doing, on trying to create another kind of psychic space in the police department, and so on. At the same point, I said "The program will be as successful as you are 'conscious' because as long as you are stuck in the polarity you're just going to enroll more people into the polarity. If you aren't stuck in the polarity you may be able to free people by the model that new policemen will have about what it is that they think they're doing every day when they go out and be policemen."

When I was in India in the temple, I was sitting there and there was a river flowing by and there were birds chirping and it was gentle and I was meditating and I felt this great feeling of well-being and calmness and I thought, "What am I doing here? Why aren't I back on the front lines? Why aren't I back fighting? Why aren't I back doing what I believe for what I believe; you know, protesting against injustice and so on? Am I copping out? Is this like a rear battle rest station? What kind of a scene am I in? Is this a cop out?" Then I began to see that staying alone in that room at that moment was confronting me with an internal battle which was much fiercer than any external battle I had ever fought before. And until I had found some way through that internal battle, all I could do was get sucked into the external manifestations of it in such a way as to perpetuate them. Right? I began to see that it was absolutely imperative in terms of socially responsible, effective behavior that I work on myself sufficiently so that I could look at any human being and see that place in them behind whatever their melodrama is, be it Nixon or a hippie or Mao or Hitler or Schweitzer or Mahatma Gandhi or whatever the person's trip is, to be able to see behind that. Until I was centered enough, till I was in that place in myself, I couldn't

39

really know that place in other beings. I saw that, finally, my responsibility was to work on myself.

Now, to bring this to the West, it seems to me that because of many of the factors that have been, I think, sufficiently well pointed out by Marshall McLuhan and others so that I don't have to particularly repeat them, there is a tremendous change in the cultural context in which we are living and it's been changing very intensively in the past ten years. This is leading to changes in our time and space concepts, the time and space concepts we live in everyday. Because of these changes we are experiencing a great input of energy. It's as if we're tuning in to more and more energy in the universe, so that you feel the geometric progression at which things are happening. Look at the culture. It's as if it's all going faster and faster and harder and harder in all directions, all at once. What I notice is that when a person feels this higher energy, which really turns out in the Hindu system to be fourth chakra, which is a place independent of time and space. When you start to experience that energy, you tend to want to "do" something with it. It's like, "I've got to do something!" And the things that you do are the habits you had out of the last trip you were on. In other words, you're on "I'm going to do something. I'm going to make this world a better place to live in. I'm going to change the system"—that's the feeling. The young persons feels, "I have all this energy. I see more. I can do it." When he starts to do something, what he ends up doing is a set of responses which are still in the third chakra, which is in the world of "we" and "them." So all he does is bring more energy to a set of old games that the culture's been playing out, where the son overthrows Daddy and then the son becomes Daddy and Daddy becomes just as bad as he was before, because he's now Daddy, see? So I can pick up a hitchhiker in Big Sur who's had to cut off his hair because he's in the army and he says, "Hey, man, this is fierce," he says, "None of the chicks will go out with me because I have short hair." And I begin to see that there's a new establishment which is the long-hair establishment. They're saying, "You can't come into our club because you don't have your credentials. You don't have an American Express Card. I'm sorry, you can't stay here."

In other words, it's a new system that comes in when that energy is used unconsciously. They're just perpetuating the illusion, perpetuating the darkness. So now it became apparent to me that what one can "do" if one feels a sense of social responsibility, which is that vector that pulls me back out of the ocean and which is what I'm doing here. One first of all keeps working on himself to become a higher and higher rate of vibration. In other words, a peaceful man is the first criterion if you want to have a peaceful universe. You start with the universe you've got, which is your own being; and if you're angry, you can't be angry about peace because all you're creating is more anger in the world, rather than more peace. So whatever you're going to do, you've got to do it peacefully. In other words, you've got to do it with peace in your heart if it has anything to do with peace. It may not, but if it has anything *really* to do with peace you've got to realize you *are* whatever it "is" and so you've got to start right there. You can't say, "Well, I'm angry about peace, and as soon as I have peace, I'll be peaceful," because it doesn't work that way. It works just the opposite because of the laws of action and reaction which the universe functions on. So you see that the only option is to work on yourself.

Increasing the Amount of Consciousness

Now does working on yourself have anything to do with whether you protest, march, drop out, drop in? No, it has nothing whatsoever to do with that, because at any moment you are consciousness involved in a nature package. That nature package includes your heredity, your environment, all of your personality characteristics, all of the opportunities that exist at this moment, all of your attitudes, all of your predispositions—the whole package. That package is functioning under the laws of karma or the laws of the universe. In other words, that package is unfolding. It's just lawfully working itself out. As you get more conscious, however, every act you perform increases the amount of consciousness in the universe, because the act itself conveys the consciousness. In other words, I could tell you the greatest truths of the world but if I don't understand them inside, forget it, because all I'm doing is taking it from there and giving it to there and I'm not giving you the key that allows you to use it, which is the "faith" in it, which I can only convey through my own success in whatever I'm doing.

So, then with all of that said, it's quite apparent that as you work on yourself, on your consciousness, you continue to do whatever dance you're doing or the dance evolves. As you are conscious, you begin to see how the acts you perform can become more and more optimum to the conditions. That is, when you're about to change a law in the country you begin to understand the way the whole system works as you stand back one bit, and you see what the optimum act you can do is, and you go and perform, and you perform it totally without the emotional attachment to that act, but with an awareness of how that act works in the whole system. You hear what I'm saying? In other words, it's the ability to sometimes have delay of gratification, if you will, the ability to stand back, to do what is the more optimum response. Sometimes it's the immediate thing to do. In other words, a parent may or may not slap the child. The parent may or may not be emotionally involved in slapping the child. The parent may or may not understand totally how many ramifications are involved in slapping the child. These are all different places which they can work at.

So finally the general rule applies to all action no matter whether you tell me that the world is going to end tomorrow or in five years or ten years or the bad guys win or the good guys win, or it's all up to me, or we've got to get together and do something. All of that leads me always to the same response: I will work on myself, since the work on myself is going to be the highest thing I can do for it all, since I understand that as man up-levels his own consciousness, he sees more creative solutions to the problems that he's confronting. Therefore, it always feeds back to the same place. But working on myself is just like this. This is social action at the moment. And yet this social action is totally without attachment. I can't be concerned with whether you can know this or not. I can only do what I do because the minute I'm concerned, I'm caught. The minute I'm caught I can only catch you.

I can tell the same thing to a black. Whether he wants to hear it or not is something else. On the West Coast I would say that I have at least 500 percent higher participation of blacks in my lectures than on the East Coast. It's as if many more of them are ready to hear this kind of information because they've begun to see the futility of their strategy. That they're going to lose what they wanted, in the bargain, with the game they're playing. Now, the matter of consciousness is how quickly you give up a past model, so that you can be here and now. In other words, the deck has now been re-dealt. The Negro is really psychologically in a different space than he was a year ago. Now, he's been oppressed for hundreds of years and he has worked very hard to get to this moment. How many years should he have to be preoccupied with how hard it was to get here? How long should that capture his consciousness? Right? In other words, I've been driving and speeding and I'm given a ticket, how long does the ticket eat away at my intestine and the acid secrete and I sit around rehearsing the thing and saying, "Well, if I had said this, and he shouldn't have done that, and I've got to fix it." Or how much, right after that, can I be here and look out and say, "Wow, look at the sun. Isn't it beautiful?" In other words, how long do I perseverate? And the black man's predicament is how long he perseverates at this point. The minute he can come into the here and now, he will appreciate that there are literally hundreds of thousands of other people around him who see him as another human being in the here and now, see blackness as a secondary rather than as a primary consideration. Is he going to spend the rest of his life punishing himself for the punishment that he has had, by retaining the paranoia, or does he give it up? The problem is one of how quick he can up-level his own predicament.

That's the question. It's for all of us the same question, you see. And all I can do to help him up-level his own predicament is for me not to get caught in it. He can say, "Look, man, you're Whitey and I'm going to beat the shit out of you." And I can say, "Yeh, baby, I understand, and here we are, right? Here we are, I understand the whole trip, why you got to do that and why you feel that, and all that; but here we are. I see it and you see it and now here we are. Now what? Now what?" And that's a fierce one. It's fierce because there are many people that are getting so many points out of their melodrama and they've been on such a thin reinforcement schedule that they don't want to give up the brownie badges they're getting. That's true of the psychoanalytic societies and it's true of blacks and it's true of the sexually beautiful women and the rich men in our society, and the handsome men. They're all getting fantastic payoffs in our externalized culture, which is not going to be enough in the long run for any of them, but they're saying, "I'll take it now even though . . ." Buddha pointed out very clearly that, just like Christ said, when he said, "Lay not up your treasures where moth and rust doth corrupt, and thieves break in and steal," Buddha said that the cause of suffering is desire or craving, and that means to be caught in time, craving things which pass. Beauty, money, power, external freedom, youth—all pass.

Therefore, any time you crave that, there is always going to be suffering built right into the situation, by definition. Even when I was going with the top models in the country, the most beautiful women in the world, I could feel in them the fear of what was going to happen tomorrow, when now they were only the second most beautiful girl in the world. That's built right into the system. It's built right into the system of time. And that's what human suffering is about—an attachment to time. What is now happening in our culture is we are having a technologically over-determined push into a place independent of time in our consciousness. We're moving to another level of consciousness. The only question is how fast we grow up to who we now are. I dig that we grow up just as fast as we are "conscious." That is, as long as communication is what it is, so everybody's hearing what everybody else is saying—fantastic amount of informational exchange—then it boils down to the most conscious beings start to help the game change. It only takes one Pasteur or one anything to change the nature of the entire dance because he touches a place where the answer is, and he brings it back, and then everybody knows it.

It is true that in the West at the moment there is a fantastic breaking down of attachment to the models that kept man locked in one particular organization of the universe. Things like nationalism, religion, racial and social-economic groups are suddenly all anachronism. And we're living with a system where to get a passport I've got to pledge undying allegiance to the United States. I'm going through something like a 1930s movie somehow because I've seen the picture they shot from the space capsule. I look at the earth and I see it's a big round sphere we're all sitting on, and any damned fool knows we're all in this thing, that's the unit we've got. As McLuhan says, "It's now the stuff that's going on in Vietnam is going on in your own back yard, because the earth is a village." And we're still saying "Now don't cross that dirt line in the center strip." It's like High Noon in an old Western, as far as I'm concerned. "That's my wheat and I can't care if you're starving."

Sure it's going to take fantastic redefinitions of all the games of energy and matter and form, and changes in institutions; but that happens just as fast as our consciousness happens. The United Nations can become an absurd joke, as it often is, where everybody's sitting in there protecting their own game, or it can shift in one moment and suddenly be a group of

45

men who are involved in a collaborative, unitive venture, if any of them can be touched by that place in each of them that is behind the ways in which they are separate—and that is based on the *Zeitgeist* or the psychic space of man at any moment. Wars effect the psychic space. When Hitler killed all those Jews, as horrible as that act lives in the world of form in Man, forever, still the service that the whole horror served was that it unified Man in the experience of the horror of it. That, in a way, brought him to a higher level of consciousness. You don't pit the giving up of a human life to any of that. I'm merely pointing out that history "is" the story. It's Man's story of evolving consciousness. That's what history is. It's always "his" story. It's not your story, it's his story. And you're living your own story. And your story will live as fast as you become conscious.

You can look around and see that the universe is being kept at the plane it is and isn't going up in smoke at the moment because when you get on the bus now and then, there's a bus driver who's so high and beautiful, that everybody that gets on his bus feels better when they get off the bus than when they get on the bus. He's just driving the bus. He just happens to be Buddha driving a bus. He's not going around saying "I'm appearing in Town Hall; I'm Buddha," see, he's just "being" Buddha. He's just doing what Buddha does. And you begin to realize that the earth is full of very high beings who are constantly spreading this other force, you know; creating this other kind of consciousness.

There's a great set of comic books called the *Dr. Strange Comics*. "Dr. Strange Meets the Mystic Mind," is one of the great ones. The Mystic Mind has created a mind net and he's not going to let anybody through. Dr. Strange has got to get through to save the Mystic Mind, who is caught in this net. So Dr. Strange sends images of himself, see, and you see Dr. Strange images going into the Mystic Mind. The Mystic Mind puts up huge nets and pushes them all back and you see their minds manifest in all of these ways—it's three dimensional. It's all comic book stuff. And then you begin to see what it means to create psychic spaces.

Drugs are a religion. I suspect people have been doing it for thousands of years, also, but they haven't been talking about it. It's quite clear now that there are what are called secret initiation rites, like the Eleusinian Mysteries and so on, secret initiation rites in many religions that are probably used or have turned out to use things like various psychedelic herbs, psychotropic herbs and so on, as part of the rite connected with it. It's entirely possible, as far as I'm concerned, psychedelics are another yoga. The fact is that at this moment we in the West don't know enough about this particular yoga, either chemically or in terms of all possible side effects and implications, or in terms of what is the optimum method to use to make it work. Those of us that are working on consciousness are looking to as many other methods as are available, to learn where we can learn from them with the idea that there is this interchange.

For example, the Good Friday study that Walter Pahnke did, that we did at Harvard and Boston University Chapel. . . . We ran twenty theological students in a double blind, placebo study on Good Friday in the Chapel, and of the ten that took the psilocybin, nine of them had a religious, mystical experience. Now they had it with psilocybin, but it's in a church, in a regular religious setting, so we're learning something about what rituals of religion are necessary for it to be a religion that brings man into the Spirit, which is what religion was supposed to be about in the first place. So it's entirely possible it can be. It behooves us to have a very, very open mind about all of this at all times. All I see is that we're exchanging information.

Do I feel I've achieved the state of mind I had before with LSD? When I am doing very formal sadhana, meaning spiritual work on myself, and part of the sadhana I do, which is part of *Ashtanga* Yoga, the yoga I pursue, involves *pranayam* which

47

is control of breath—control of pran through breathing techniques. Under these conditions I have gone into states that are comparable to almost all of the states I have experienced with LSD, not all of them but almost all of them. I see that that is a method very similar, in certain ways, in that it forces, it overrides, certain habits of thought and places I'm not, in order to put me in that place, and then I come back from it. It's a discontinuous place again for me. But it functions very much like psychedelics and you can get hooked on pranayam in the same way you can get hooked on the experience of LSD. All of them are experiences. And, you finally have to give up experiencing it to *be* it, and then you're beyond the psychedelic or beyond the *Hatha* Yoga or the pranayam.

This is an interesting situation for me here, because gathered together here are not only members of the Menninger family but members of the—I don't know how to say it—the hippie community, the young people, the long hairs, the "problems" that our society faces, the drop-outs, the young seekers, the people who don't have a vested interest in the game, the ones that are letting the change happen, the people that are on the firing line that are doing it rather than thinking about it. There are a lot of different levels at which we can define who we are here this evening. It's quite easy to take a group of very high hippies and go out until we're all just beyond words together. It's quite easy to sit down to a psychiatric staff conference.

Recently I spoke at the Einstein Medical School to the psychiatric Grand Rounds. There was a long conference table and I came in with my beads and my whole business and the psychiatrists all sat around the table. This was usually a case conference. And I looked into their eyes and into their hearts and I knew that I was the case. There was no doubt about it. Although the little program said I was the guest speaker, that was obviously a misprint. I was sitting cross-legged on the end of the conference table, which is because that's the most comfortable for me. And I'm working with my beads. And I look like that poor Dr. Alpert that used to be at Harvard and took all those drugs and look at what we . . . this is a very interesting case this week, and you know . . . well, he's schizophrenic, you know. And I had heard all that. I used to sit in case conferences for many years.

So, I presented myself as a case. I talked about the onset of hallucination and the dissociative experiences and I reported my whole journey in psychodynamic terms, just as if I were the doctor on the case presenting the case. It took a couple of minutes before it became apparent to everybody that the patient was presenting himself, which is an unusual situation, for the patient to present the Freudian dynamics, etc., right? Now in the whole course of it I only used terms like "religion," "God" and "spirit" in terms of talking about the patient's responses. And when I talked about *mandala* I talked about a heuristic device for cognitive centering because I found out the truth could be said in whatever metaphor we need, to communicate with one another. If the message is pure enough it should be able to be said to everybody so that everybody can hear it in the way they need to hear it. The interesting experience for all of us tonight was to be able to bridge all those funny little gaps that we're all stuck in, saying I'm me and there's them and there's them here and them here, which were in my head as well, and find a way of answering each question so that there is the optimum possibility that all of us can hear what we need to hear. And I realize that this demands work on myself that is extraordinary, that I haven't yet done enough of, but it's the kind of work I'm doing, because if I am pure enough, in how I understand it, I will be nobody, and what will come out of my mouth will be a function of all the consciousnesses gathered in this room at the moment. What will come out will be the optimum thing needed for all these consciousnesses. So that's been the experiment we've been playing with tonight and I've found it.

MODIFICATION OF GROUP CONSCIOUSNESS

Once one sees how these processes work, one sees that what we have just been doing is as formal and disciplined an intensive device to change consciousness, when entered into freely, as any other technique. And the repetition of simple phrases and the use of a drone instrument such as this one here is a quite exquisitely designed vehicle. In a number of seminars, week-long seminars I've run at growth centers, at Esalen, for example, I have created a psychic space, a certain environment. We've all lived together for five days, cooked together, in silence, using chalk boards. Part of our work involved doing all-night chanting where with drums and cymbals and tamboura and flutes we would just repeat "Rama" or "Hari Krishna" or whatever phrase we were working with. Just do it over and over and over again. We'd go through change after change after change in terms of the group consciousness. You go through the excitement, enthusiasm, the boredom, the fatigue, and keep going on and on and on behind that. Finally you get into a space where the thing is going on by itself. It is as if it's a wheel and ball bearings, and everybody's just sort of doing that thing to keep it going. It's this place we have all come into where we are now the keepers of the song rather than having all the little separate games we brought to it. And it becomes a very, very high vehicle for group consciousness modification.

The Problem of the Experimenter

How much can one remain an experiment? I think that there is a part of the process that involves giving up any specific predisposition you have. There is an act of surrender. Now it turns out that when you give it up you don't lose it like you thought you were going to do when you gave it up, but you do have to give it up. I consider myself data, really. I consider myself a subject in the world of Western science because my own consciousness is the stuff and I can only be studied within the subject-object world of the experimenter by someone independent of me, since it's happening to me. At the same time, I was trained as an experimental social scientist and therefore what I'm doing now is really a behavioristic study of my own behavior change . . . or my own change. Did you make it through?

We got so frightened of Titchenerian Introspectionism in

the way we got into Behaviorism that we got fiercely into Behaviorism, and we ruled out the possibility that a person could be the observer of his own behavior, without having the subjective fallacy as the experimenter. There are ways of training yourself to do this, once you stop being afraid to do it, and it is a body of knowledge that becomes available that way. It doesn't meet the criterion of being public data, but it still fulfills certain criteria and as such is a body of knowledge not formally within the scientific system. There are parts of this where the model of being an experimenter stands in your way. There is no doubt about that. It corrupts it. You have to give up being the experimenter to have the experience of the transcendence of experimenter-ness. And this is one of the problems: you can only know you know after you've been it . . . and in order to be it you've got to give up knowing you know. It's a fantastic paradox.

LIMITATIONS OF KNOWING

How do you reconcile faith and reason? Well, as I feel it now, we have come out of a period where in the evolutionary journey of us as beings, Man evolves these great frontal lobes and this capacity for rational thought or for self-consciousness. And this is, in the Hindu system, what would be called *siddhi* or a power. That power can be used in a variety of ways. It can be used in the service of what I call the third chakra, that is, in terms of man's control over his environment, which is the way we've been doing it, which the rational mind controls. It's man over nature in the anthropological Florence Kluckhohn differentiations. She talks about societies that are man *over* nature, societies that are man *in* nature, and societies that are man *under* nature. Attachment to the siddhi of the rational mind put man in the group of man over nature. That particular way of knowing the world through the rational mind has tremendous advantages, obviously, which we have exploited as hard as we could. At the same point, it is becoming apparent that there are certain limitations to that particular device for knowing. That is, that it is in "time" . . . it is in "time." It takes an ob-

51

ject and it cannot get beyond the subject-object world, the rational mind can't. It can't know itself; it's a metasystem. It is linear, for the most part and, therefore, it is tremendously limited in dealing with large numbers of variables simultaneously. Even the high-powered computer doesn't approximate.

Now it turns out, that there are ways of knowing the universe which for the most part we have relegated to the realm of mysticism, or poetry, or romantic poetry, or falling in love. We sometimes call it "intuitive validity" in science. That's the closest we get to it. There are ways of knowing about things that we don't know through our analytic, rational mind. But since we have committed ourselves, we have grown up. In order to survive we have become participants in a religion. If a religion is a specific faith, the faith is, faith in the rational mind. And, therefore, we as professors or as rationalists become the priests in that particular faith system, which is a faith, after all. It's faith in the fact that what you know through your senses, through your thinking mind, and through the logic of your thinking mind, that that has anything to do with anything. That's a faith. There's nothing you can do about it, because you can never get outside of the predicament of knowing, independent of that faith.

Now once you begin to experience that man is caught in a dilemma, that his vehicle is finite and he's trying to know something about the infinite, and you begin to realize that right over the hill from Plank's constant is something pretty interesting, but that you can never get there with your rational mind, you begin to entertain what William James has talked about as altered states of consciousness, which are not primarily experiencing information through the linear, analytic process of what we call logical, rational process. Now a lot of the techniques for altering consciousness take you into states where you are experiencing a relationship to what was previously what you'd call the objective universe, in such a way that you are experiencing it in a *subjective* rather than an objective sense. In other words, you are experiencing a unitive link with it rather than knowing through your senses. It is known in the mystic trade as the opening of the third eye, which people have related to the pineal gland and so on, which is probably just more stuff to feed into your computer to confuse you. But whatever it is, it is very clear that there are ways of knowing that are not knowing either through your senses or through your rational mind.

Whether or not that way of knowing is useful to man is something that we only know as we explore and enter into that realm ourselves, you see. Now, it turns out that what is required to get to the next level of consciousness is to transcend the rational mind. That means to transcend the knower who knows. And that is a very frightening thing when that has been your vehicle for controlling your universe up until that point. And it turns out, of course, that when you do that you end up *with* your rational mind but in the role of a servant rather than a master. We're coming out of that place, as I said last night, of *cogito, ergo sum* and we're now going into a place where we're seeing that we aren't our thinking mind but that it is merely another servant, not the master.

EVOLVING CONSCIOUSNESS

I cannot see it all as but summating. That is, I feel that I am somebody who has been in a way blessed by having been given everything that Western society could offer, in large part, in terms of affluence, so that I was not concerned about my security, so I could finish with that; lots of love from people around me; the best training, with a Ph.D. and that kind of a research orientation; the best technology could offer me in terms of transportation, communication, psychedelics, and life process; and I feel that all that was part of my preparation to now know something else, to do something else. I don't see it any more particularly as Eastern versus Western. I merely see this as a logical progression of my own evolving consciousness. And I see the way it's happening to me is quite Western. I am making use of Eastern methods. I am not Hindu. I am a Western, Jewish boy from Boston who has studied Hinduism. I also find the same thing in the Greek Orthodox Christians, and in the Hasidic movement in Judaism. I find it in all mystical traditions: in the Sufi, in the Egyptian, and certainly in St. Teresa and St. John and so on. So that, I find that it is in a way the amalgam of all this stuff that is allowing me to be what I am doing right at this moment.

It seems to me that there was a point where my "attachment" to my Western training stood in my way. I didn't have to give up my Western training, what I had to give up was my "attachment" to my Western training. That's the critical difference. I didn't lose my Western training. As I said last night, Jung said in a eulogy of Richard Wilhelm, "He is a gnostic intermediary, in that he was willing to give up a Western predisposition in order to experience another system at the being-level, in order to bring it back." Now my bringing it back is as a Western scientist. And all that stuff is helping me be able to translate it into something that is meaningful to us in the West at this moment in the work we're doing. I see that as tremendously valuable. But I do see that my "attachment" to my rational mind at one point was an impediment, although the "development" that I have with my rational mind is clearly an asset. The power of the rational mind . . . that particular siddhi, as it's called in the Hindu system—when you turn that back in on itself, which is called *Jnana* Yoga or the Yoga of the Rational Mind Beating Itself—which is part of the Zen Koan and so on, demand exquisite discipline of the rational mind. That, in a way, was usable only because of the disciplines I had developed. So that I see them very much as an amalgam rather than in any kind of sense as contradictory.

The truth is everywhere. Wherever you are, it's right where you are, when you can see it. And you can see it through whatever vehicle you are working with, you can free yourself from certain attachments that keep you from seeing it. The scientist doesn't stop being a scientist, nor anybody stop being anything. You find how to do the things to yourself which allow you to find truth where you are at that moment. I'd say we never find out anything new; we just remember it.

two

MEHER BABA AND BHAKTI YOGA

Meher Baba was an Indian holy man who was a very pure, pure statement of Bhakti Yoga, the Yoga of Devotion, the Yoga of Love. The heart is a vehicle for transcendence. The relation between lover and beloved that I was talking about before. He left his body about a year ago. He died. And to the extent that one reads his discourses and his books like *A God Speaks* or *Listen Humanity!* with the openness of the fourth chakra, with love in one's heart, he is a very, very high teacher. There's no doubt about that. I've had very powerful spiritual contacts with Meher Baba and I feel that he is one of my gurus, one of the beings that guide my unfolding. And he pointed out to me in correspondence, when he was in his body, that he thought that there was a problem in relation to LSD— that you became addicted to the experience of LSD rather than working for the true reality. I have come to understand what he meant by that, over the years, as I've gone on in my own work. I feel that he's just a very loving being who is there for people that can open their hearts to him.

EDGAR CAYCE AND TWO STATES OF CONSCIOUSNESS

Edgar Cayce, it seems to me, was a being who had available to him what William James calls the discontinuity of two states of consciousness. He could move from one state of consciousness into the other. However, he did not have recall of one from the other. He didn't have it "all together," as we

55

would say in the West. So he would go into a sleep state, where he would be in another state of consciousness where he would see the universe differently than he was seeing it in another state, and see more than was available to him when he was in his waking consciousness. I think that's all valid and that what he was reporting was what he was seeing at that astral plane, which is a relatively low astral plane, as far as I can see . . . and was open to certain influences and so on. It's not perhaps a totally pure statement, but it's a very good statement. It's certainly more than we knew before. It is another way of defining reality. And James' point is well taken. Any premature closing of our accounts with reality which fails to take into account all of these other states of consciousness is an error on man's part because man has to be pretty pompously presumptuous to assume that he's already found out the way. And so, you take a person like Edgar Cayce and it is difficult because of the sort of shucky nature of the organization that got going around him, often to hear the wisdom of the message in there and to hear the real stuff in there. But there certainly is a lot of real stuff in there. There's no doubt about it.

It's like when you get to a certain point you can start to read the Bible as a very high manual, a text, a manual for work on yourself in consciousness. When Christ is talking about, "He that is born of flesh is flesh; he that is born of spirit" . . . and "that ye be born again, ye must die and be reborn." Things like, "I and my father are one." You can take almost all of the stuff and find immediately how it is relating to what process we are going through at this moment. I find that once you are open to new possibilities. . . . I see that the problem we're all afraid of, especially scientists, is opening Pandora's Box. We're afraid if we let something in sloppily, somehow we're going to drown in our own, you know. What we better decide is, "Is Edgar Cayce good? Is Meher Baba good? Should I listen to him? Should I?"—as if we're protecting our virginity somehow. Well, it turns out that one of the things that has to be surrendered is that model. You've got to have enough faith to allow it all to come in, with the idea that that which is truth will rise to the surface. The scientific mold is to listen to something sitting back, listening to it, saying, "Shall I believe it or not?" The other way of doing it is to open yourself to it, embrace it, and become it; and if it is inappropriate it will spew itself out. But that takes a certain kind of faith that is very, very scary if you think you have to sit in this protected place, and the predicament is that a person who's saying, "Shall I allow that to be known or not by me? Shall I consider this as another part of reality?" is cutting himself off from knowing it by the nature of his mechanism. He can't know it that way. That's the problem. He can't know the stuff in that objective sense. He's got to embrace it. He has got to make love with the unknown. He's got to enter into a love relationship with the unknown, risky though that woman may be because she's got a lot of weird foibles. And you've got to make love with her with the total faith that if your intent is pure, the thing will be O.K. The truth will out. And you've finally got to get off your place you're standing on. That's part of what we are talking about tonight: that ability to risk your position. "You've got to risk it all to have it all"—as these old saws out of the mystical literature tell you. You've got to give it all up to have it all. Very far out! You've got to give it all up to have it all.

FEAR AND HIGHER STATES OF CONSCIOUSNESS

Would I say something about what man fears he will see if he risks all? Well, generally I think that the first level of fears are concerned with that part of us which is in nature, that Freud talks about—the unconscious impulses. And I think that there is a fear that if one lets go of rational control, surrenders that, one will be animal-like in the sense of antisocial impulses. I think that's the first fear—that there are things in oneself that are ugly, untenable, unsociable, and so on. That's part of the fear, part of one's own animal. This is because one doesn't go back far enough, as far as I can see. Because if you go one step behind that, you see something else in man behind that one, too. And then that's just another melodrama. The fear is, at the first chakra, the loss of the separate entity, the loss of one's individuality, the loss of one's identity, the psychological dying, the loss of the experiencer or the knower. That's part of what that fear is. Another part of the fear is that you may start to go out and only get part way, and get stuck somewhere else that will be worse than this one. That's another fear which is called "eternal damnation," when in fact *this is* eternal damnation, for people who are experiencing eternal damnation. And eternal damnation is just another trip. Send them through eternal damnation for a while is more like where eternal damnation is at. It is . . . fear is perhaps a frontward or a front emotional reaction for man's lack of readiness to deal with the higher energy states and higher input and output that is connected with these other states of consciousness. The fear is a protective mechanism in the sense that he experiences a kind of free-floating anxiety or ambiguous fear about it. And that keeps him from getting too close to it. He isn't ready, or able to get close to it because he can't do the necessary things to be able to live in those states of consciousness without doing destructive things to himself. He's not pure enough.

I think fear is the result of impurity. And impurity means, thoughts that define oneself in a "profane" sense, that is, thoughts which define oneself as separate. And as long as you are attached to those thought forms, you are going to fear, because it involves the extinction of that separate being, that separate conceptual entity.

I'll deal with questions very gently and talk around them for a while so don't keep holding your hand up because we all have questions. We're all here together. It's all our questions of ourselves. And what we don't ask we already know the answers to anyway so it's all right. It's only a little dance we're doing, anyway. We shouldn't take it too seriously.

In my experience in guiding people through LSD experiences, there is the fear that many people experience as this chemical transformation occurs in their bodies and which leads them to the breakdown of all existing models that they had about how the universe works. As that happens there are many people who experience intense fear, which makes them want to hold onto the structure they had. And they could say, "I am afraid, I am going insane," meaning I am going into another space that I don't have any control over on this level. In general I would say, "Well, groovy, let's go insane together. Here we go." In other words, it is my feeling that the only thing you have to fear is fear, in that sense that to the extent that you have enough faith or trust to let it happen, you always go through the next one and the next one and the next one.

In the Tibetan literature they say, "Embrace your ten thousand horrible demons and your ten thousand beautiful demons." You've just got to take it all and keep going. "Yeah, that one too," and "That one too," and keep going. All your fears have to be embraced, entertained, honored, and you go on with them.

There is a qualitative difference in my life now from ten years ago, in that I do not experience a fear of death as a real fear when I get into situations where death seems a possibility, or violence, or something like that. I don't have any of the usual or earlier kinds of reactions of anxiety or fear and yet I do what is adaptive to protect the temple or body I'm working with. But I don't do it out of fear, because the fear of death seems somehow to have flown the coop somewhere along the way in this game. It certainly changes the nature of my living experience every day because each day can be whatever it is, and it's all all right. I'm not collecting something to avoid something later.

LOVE AS A STATE OF BEING

If a Western man were to become a fully enlightened being what would happen to his human relationships, particularly love? Let me start with the word "love" for a moment. I think there is a transformation that goes on in one's conception of the term "love." And I think one changes from seeing it as a verb, to seeing it as a state of being. And you move much more toward what would be called Christ-love, that is, the state of being where one "is" love. One is like a light that emits, and one is a loving being. Consciousness and energy are an identity, as I said last night, and similarly with those identities is the term love. That is, that love and consciousness are one and the same thing. So that as you get into a higher state of consciousness you come closer to being in love. That doesn't mean in interpersonal love. It means being—love. Now if you and I love or fall into love and I say, "She really turns me on. I love her," from this model what I see is happening is that I'm saying, "You are a . . . ," in the imprinting literature, "You are a superordinate key stimulus that is eliciting an innate response mechanism. You're releasing an innate response mechanism." Or I could say it in a more general sense, saying that, "You're turning me on." And you're turning me on to a place inside myself that is love. So I am experiencing what it means to "be in love." And I'm saying I am in love with you. I am in love with my connection to the place in me that is love, is the way I would now say it in this Western framework. Now to keep working with this I would say that as you are making love and getting totally into interpenetration as much as your bodies would allow and your thoughts and feelings would often allow and still feel that there was a separateness. And it is interesting that as long as you are under the illusion that what you are loving is "out there," you will always experience that separateness.

It is only when you begin to understand that if you and I are truly in love, if I go to the place in me that is love and you to the place in you that is love, we are "together" in Love. We start to understand that what love means is that we are sharing a common state together. That state exists in you and it exists in me. Now the enlightened being—what happens to him is that he changes the nature of his love object from a specific love object to it all, finally. You would say that an enlightened being is totally in love with the universe, in the sense

60

that everything in the universe turns him on to that place in himself where he is love and consciousness. So I would say that an interpersonal relationship that has any qualities of possessiveness in it, or ego drama of any kind, certainly undergoes changes as the nature of consciousness changes. And at the same moment I would say that as a person becomes more conscious, he understands that he has certain karmic commitments, that is, existing contracts which may be with parents, it may be with husband or wife, it may be with children— and that he cannot rid himself from these without creating a karmic cost—without leaving behind him some uncooked seeds that he's running away from.

The game of enlightenment starts from exactly where you are at this moment, and therefore, if you have an existing social-emotional-sexual contract with another human being, that's where it starts. To say, "Well, I've got to go do my work on myself. I can't afford you any more" leaves a ripping which ultimately you've got to rectify. There's no doubt about it. You've got to work from where you are now. You just can't walk away from anything, any part of your life. You've got to bring it all into harmony at every new level.

I am in India and I suddenly realize that I have to come back. My mother has died, I have to come back and be with my father in a new way than I was ever with him before. To share that particular drama, I don't think I shared my father last night, did I? When I came back to Boston from India, I arrived at the airport and I was wearing a beard and I was barefoot, and I had come from India with my tamboura and I was generally a weird-looking being. My father came in his car to pick me up—as I said, a conservative Boston Republican and a very responsible member of our society. He took one look at me, and his response was, "Get in quick before anybody sees you," which I did, and we started to drive toward the house. Now what he regaled me with all the way home was the fact that he was experiencing a depression, a deep depression, as he approached death. He was seventy-two at the time. He told me all about how his life was meaningless and even though he had started Brandeis University, and raised many funds for The Einstein Medical School, and been President of the New Haven Railroad, and done lots of glorious and grand things in his life—he was experiencing the feeling that he was a failure as a human being. That was all there was to it. And he was telling me about his will and the clauses in his will, and all I felt was . . . I was sitting in the car doing my *Om Mani Padme Hum, Om Mani Padme Hum.* And it was like his mind was creating this huge big black cloud of pollution in the car; I mean, this heavy, dark depressed place of "it's all over" and "we'll look through the old photographs tonight"—you know that kind of place. And I just did my mantra and off we drove to the house.

We got home and he said, "What would you like to do now?" I said, "I don't care, Dad, anything you'd like to do." He said, "Well, I want you to rest. You've had a long trip and. . . ." He said, "I'm going to make some raspberry jam," because that's one of his hobbies, is making raspberry jam. So I said, "Well, can I help you?" "No, don't bother." I said, "I'd like to." He said, "All right." So I go in, and we start to make raspberry jam. We're sterilizing the bottles and mashing raspberries, and he's telling me about the horror of his life and how sad it is, and how everybody's forgotten him and, boy, he's got a routine. It's a very heavy story, very heavy story. I feel fantastic compassion for him because I love him very dearly and at the same moment I see the predicament his consciousness is in. I see where he's stuck. So I'm just doing my mantra and mashing raspberries and so on, and I'm saying to him things like, "Should the bubbles all rise to the top? Are the bottles right? Where do we put that?" and so on. And after a while, since I'm giving him no reinforcement at all for this fantastic dark cloud that he's creating and holding all by himself, since I'm part of us, but I'm not helping him hold it up particularly, he starts to say, "Well, get all the bubbles up . . ." and pretty soon his conversation is shifting until it's in the here and now.

That is, he's talking about how to make raspberry jam, right? And as he starts to talk about how to make raspberry jam— this is a technique you're all familiar with of bringing a person into the here and now—the lines of his face are relaxing and the whole model of himself as somebody who's old and about to die and his life is lived out and all this stuff about his failures and unhappiness and bankruptcy of the railroad and all that stuff, that's all sort of falling into the past and here we are making raspberry jam. We're just two guys making raspberry jam, right? Now we finish making the raspberry jam, and he's happy, see, he's smiling.

So now his question is, "What are we going to do together next?" Right? Because what's happening is he's getting a "contact high" off me, because I'm living in the here and now. All I'm doing is making raspberry jam. And he's coming into that place, and it feels good. Everyone wants to feel good. He's coming into that place, and he feels good. If I walk away for an hour or two, he'll go right back into that other space again, because that's his karma at that moment to be stuck still in that space. But we start to spend a great deal of time together and as we spend more and more time together, he's living more in the here and now.

To short-cut the whole story, let me explain that eight months later, I gave the bride away at his marriage. Right? He married a woman in her early fifties, a beautiful, high, wonderful woman who had actually been one of his secretaries in the Junior Achievement organization, of which he was president. There was another Junior Achievement for him. As he went into the temple, he said to me, "This is all your doing, you know," because what I did was hold his hand all the time because all of his questions would be about the future or the past, like, "Is this wrong in terms of the memory of Mother? Is this going to be a terrible thing later?" All I was saying was, "How does it feel today? Did you have a good time at dinner last night? What are we doing today?" And he said, "Oh, it's wonderful. She's a wonderful person, but I'm just concerned about . . ." As soon as his mind stopped creating all that stuff about then and then, and he lived here and now, it was a gas. He was having a ball. He was writing love songs and they went on a honeymoon in Scotland and Ireland. She is a very high being, in that she lives in the here and now very much of the time. She's a very conscious being. He married a good one. He's in good hands. And when I call, I say, "What are you doing?" "Oh, well, we're . . ." and he sort of laughs, "we're writing some songs at the piano. We're writing some movie routines. We're going to shoot some sound movies and, you know, have some people over." He's having a ball. He's . . . he is no more seventy-four now. Before he was ninety-six and now he's about twenty-three, the way I figure it. And he can't walk as well and he's slowing down in all his processes but there they are. The depression has fallen away because he's started to live in the here and now. Now that's part of how consciousness affected the nature of a love relationship in a sense.

My relationship with my father was a love relationship. He is karmically my father, that is, in this incarnation he is my father. Otherwise, I don't think he and I would have much going with one another. Because he lives in a very different psychological space from the one I do. He has this big estate in New Hampshire and he's a member of this club called the President's Club. It's made up of people like presidents of United States Steel and Bell Telephone and they sit around saying, "You're a president, I'm a president. . . ." It's a status reward for having made it in the game, you know. It's an inner club and they play games together. It's beautiful. So they come up to visit him and then he'll always say things like, "I've got this son. He's a little strange, but I'd really like you to hear him." And then he'll say, "Rich," or he calls me "Rum Dum," actually. "Rum Dum, would you come down and visit?" And I come down and I sit by the fire and I tell ghost stories. I mean I talk about the weird and the beyond the beyond and strange experiences in the Himalayas—the farthest reaches of the Himalayas, you know. And as long as it's not threatening,

64

everybody's having a ball, you know: "fascinating, absolutely wonderful." And my father, who's listened to the story probably a hundred times now, always sits in the same armchair, and about ten o'clock he pushes himself up out of the chair and says, "Well, damned interesting." He says, "Don't understand a word of it, but if he's doing it, it's O.K. with me. I guess I'll turn in now." And he always does the same routine. And I know that he is just not ready or interested, or at all involved in hearing the conceptualization or the ability to work with this stuff, but nevertheless the spin-off is very much part of his daily life. I feel that this is a very subtle way in which karma works, and that we have dealt here with a matter of how consciousness changes, because my father and I are closer than we have ever been in our lives together. We genuinely and openly love one another now, in this way. I see the game of father and son as merely another social role relationship. We don't have any biological function at the moment, but we do have a karmic connection. And I honor him as my father. The result is, we're very close, and we're not hung up in all the melodramas we always were before.

THE I CHING

I think *The I Ching* is a very, very high statement of how it all is and it can be used very cautiously and consciously to wake you up to other perspectives of where you're at in the here and now. I tend less to use it as an oracular book than as a statement of the here and now, of where you're at this moment in your consciousness when you're asking the question that you're asking of *The I Ching*. As such it's very useful for up-leveling the melodrama you were caught in, to ask the question in the first place.

DIET AND FOOD

When you are working on consciousness, just like I said that the kind of breath you have, the intensity of your breath, becomes part of the environment in which you are doing your work, so, too, the entire constitution of your body becomes part of the environment in which you're doing the work. In the Hindu system this would be known as the temple in which you are residing while you're working on yourself in this round. And the nature of the constitution of the temple, the vibrational nature of it, has something to do with the ease with which you can bring your consciousness into other states. That is, your body can bring you down. Now, your body, if it fidgets and is agitated, brings you down and therefore the whole business of developing a clear seat, or *asan*, through Hatha Yoga, is part of that process of getting your body cooled-out so it will stay in the same place for awhile. That's just one of the reasons. So, what you eat starts to affect the nature of your attitudes and feelings.

In India, foods are divided into three categories, which are called *Tamasic, Rajasic,* and *Sattvic,* and since the Hindu system is based on concern with consciousness we can listen to it with a certain kind of thoughtfulness. Of these three forces in the universe, the Tamasic one is like inertia, toward "rockness" or toward the inert, the Rajasic force is like that of fire, toward action and movement, and the Sattvic force is that which is toward consciousness. There are certain foods that are called Sattvic foods, other foods which are called Rajasic foods, and still other foods which are called Tamasic foods. And it is suggested that when you are working on consciousness you eat primarily Sattvic foods. Now Sattvic foods turn out to be primarily—various books describe them differently and list different ones—primarily limiting oneself to fruits, honey, nuts, dairy products. As you go on into this work deeper and deeper, you sensitize your body through various asans, opening certain nerves through meditation, through pranayam, and your diet keeps changing. You get into lighter and lighter diets until finally you start to move toward giving up the grains and the wheats and moving toward fruits and nuts and milk and things like that. And pretty soon you get into primarily fruits, and so on. Now, you can't go on one of these diets in a crash program when you're not ready to be on it, because unless you're at a certain degree of purity, your body needs other things. And so all of the World Health Organization standards about what are the protein requirements, and so on, are all true for a Western man who is thinking like a Western man. As you change your nature of consciousness in terms of thought forms, and as you change your environment, then the kinds of foods you need change as well. Right? I don't eat meat, fish, chicken, or eggs. I don't eat them because I am in a situation where I meet people in India who know how it is and they say, "Look we don't eat them," and so I don't eat them because I'm a copy cat because I want what they've got. That's the reason I don't eat them. I can't give you a very hip, sophisticated, rational model.

I'm not going to give you a model in terms of killing, because it is true that even in the act of killing, if it can be done without attachment, it does not create karma. You can eat animal flesh if you can do it without attachment. If you're a realized being, you can eat anything and convert it. If you're not a realized being, whatever you eat affects who you are. Some of the rationale that is extant in the temple I was living in about meat, for example, is that the animal kingdom has a rudimentary type of self-consciousness and experiences some kinds of fear, rudimentary types of fear, at the moment of death. This fear releases certain kinds of adrenalin substances into the flesh of the animal and when you eat them these substances affect your constitution, no matter how they are transmuted through cooking and so on. And while it is true that there is research showing that plants show electrical reactions to being cut down and anticipation and all that, we don't know that that is the same thing as pain or fear or suffering. All we know is that these are electrical reactions. It may be the reaction of fear that is forced in, which releases adrenalin, which gives one that agitated rajasic quality that meat is connected with in the West. As you're getting into a more meditative life, you start to eat more meditative food. So I used to be on the macrobiotic diet and now I am not. I have some reservations about it and about the wisdom of George Osawa's theories, and so on. I feel there is truth in that as there is truth in everything. There was truth in Newtonian physics even though it was slightly off because it wasn't Einsteinian. It's all part of how it all is, which is unknowable. The Vedas refer to keeping a diet of bland grains and milk and fruits and things like that. And I think that you keep getting simpler and simpler.

Now it turns out that what we know about the human possibility is so absurdly trivial thus far. A woman like Teresa Neumann, the Christian mystic, has lived for twelve years eating one eucharist wafer every morning and those are mighty thin, I'll tell you—and that's it. She's a good healthy woman, a *saftig medchen* with flesh on her bones and all that. The scientists have followed her into the bathroom to see how she's cheating because they can't do it. And when they say to her, "What do you live on?" she says, "I live on light." Now, we can't do photosynthesis because we don't know how to do it and because we're busy being somebody who works a certain way. Now that doesn't say anything about Man's possibilities. Once you find one person whom you could let in the doorway without thinking there's a lie or a deception or "I'm being hustled" because "I can't do it," you begin to see that there are extraordinary other possibilities in terms of what a person needs for life force other than what we think of as the minimum daily requirements. The whole picture starts to change. There are beings that live on less and less. And as you do this purification you indeed live on less and less.

PERCEPTUAL VANTAGE POINTS AND PSYCHOSIS

I feel the resonance of all the past words that have been said about that in this room. I'm sure I could find something in here to resonate with. We live at a plane of reality which we share, it would seem, in which we all agree that certain things are the way they are. And when somebody disagrees with that and disagrees with it with deep faith, under certain conditions we characterize that as psychosis. I would now reinterpret that

68

and say that what has happened is, that the person—and this is not yet saying anything more, it's merely giving us a framework to see an alternative possibility—has moved from one perceptual vantage point to another. A person, through something which might be a chemical change, could be in a trauma of some sort; it might be ingested, or psychically induced, psychogenic in nature—but through some trauma to the system— he moves from one perceptual vantage point to another one, and then gets as attached to that one as we are to the one we're in. Right? He is attached to that and from our point of view he is psychotic. From his point of view, we are. That is because we don't see reality as he sees it. He's seeing another reality. In any kind of a Hindu system this would be called merely an astral plane. He's in another astral plane.

This morning I was talking with one of the psychiatrists here on the staff, and I was telling him about my brother who has been in a mental hospital, who has been considered psychotic, who thinks of himself as the Messiah, and with whom I have spent a great deal of time, since I have as much a karmic link to him as to my father and whatever this consciousness is all about, it must have something to do with my brother, too. And my relation to him was to be as much "here and now" as I could be just as I had been with my father. To realize that he is stuck in a reality, just like my father is, just like I get stuck, and that any reality you're stuck in is just as bad as any other reality you're stuck in. And so, one of the things I do is I go into the reality he's stuck in with him. I look around, enjoy it with him, look at the world from that place with him, and then show him that from my point of view, you have to be able to go in and out of all of them, that any one you get stuck in is the wrong one. And if one guy's stuck in one who may be a psychiatrist, he is trying to cure somebody else stuck in another and is, in one sense, just substituting one stuckness for another stuckness. The journey of consciousness is to go to the place where you see that all of them are really relative realities and these are merely perceptual vantage points for looking at it all. When one looks at the universe from within the spirit, which is another "take," one sees that the entire universe all makes absolutely exquisite sense, but it's all slightly different because you're looking at it from an entirely different perceptual vantage point.

There are some beings that we call psychotic who in India would be called "God-Intoxicants." They are people who are primarily preoccupied with the fifth chakra at this moment. That is, they are beings who have experienced compassion outwardly and then their entire energy turns inward to inner states that they are experiencing. We see them as catatonic. That would be usually the category we would see them in. Because we are not getting an elicited response out of them, we project into them a certain kind of psychological state. Now in India they project another kind of interpretation into that, surround the person with another environment, which changes the nature of his experience, because of their models of what it is that's happening to him, you see? So that a God-Intoxicant is treated with great reverence and respect. Ramakrishna, a very famous mystic in India, was often God-Intoxicant. I would say that probably most catatonics are not God-Intoxicants, but there are some that we're confusing, and we've got them in the same category because we don't have these differentiations at this point.

Another Karmic Relationship

My further understanding is that there is no being at any state of consciousness that one cannot make contact with, if one is himself free of attachment to any specific plane of consciousness. That is, I think that all of us are available at all times. There is a place in all of us that is available at all times, and our inability to make contact with another human being is our own inability to get out of the place we are stuck in. There is much to say for the flexibility of the consciousness of the behavior change agent, to be able to make contact with another human being where he is, without themselves getting stuck in

70

where he's stuck. That's the work on one's self. My brother was producing voluminous amounts of material, reading Greek, which he had never been able to read before. He was doing a number of phenomenal things which the doctors saw as pathological—his agitation, the fact that he could steal, lie, and cheat and tell that he was Christ. He escaped from the hospital a number of times, a very creative fellow.

My reading of his materials showed me that he was tuned in on some of the greatest truths in the world that have ever been enunciated by some of the highest beings. He was experiencing these directly, but he was caught in a feeling that this was happening only to him. In other words, he had taken an ego with him into this other state of consciousness and he was experiencing it as unique to himself. And, therefore, he got into a messy predicament of saying, "I've been given this, and you haven't," you see. As we decided to share time and space, he noted that everything he said on this level I understood, and we could talk at this level together, although the psychiatrist sitting in the room was having a very difficult time dealing with this visitor who was obviously crazier than the patient, you know. And my brother often said to me, "I don't know," he says, "I'm a lawyer, I'm a decent citizen, I've got a tie and a jacket, and I go to church, and I'm a good person, and I read the Bible. Me they've got in a mental hospital; you, you walk barefoot, you've got a beard, you've got a funny name, you really wear . . . you, you're out, free. How do you explain that?" And I say, "Well, I'll show you how." I said, "Do you think you're Christ? the Christ in pure consciousness?" He says, "Yes." I say, "Well, I think I am too." And he looks at me and he says, "No, you don't understand." I say, "That's why they lock you up," you see. Because the minute you tell somebody else they're not Christ, they lock you up. The minute you say, "I am and you're not," then you gotta go. It's very clear. That's the way the game is played. As far as I'm concerned, we're all God. Here we all are. Now I don't go around forcing you to say "You are God, aren't you?" Because you only come to somebody else when you are caught in an ego drama, when you are caught having to "do" something. I said to him, "If you didn't have to do anything to anybody else, nobody would put you away." The funny play . . . the reason they put him away, which was just so cosmically humorous, was that my father, a Republican, conservative, came into my brother's apartment and found him sitting there naked, surrounded by five or six elderly ladies who were worshipping him. And he was sitting there burning his money and his credit cards. In a Jewish middle-class family you can do everything, but you don't burn the money, I'll tell you . . . so that anybody could see that he was obviously crazy.

Now if you happen to be a very deeply religious student you would understand exactly what was going on on quite another level, you see, and the humor of it is very far out . . . and the compassion and the poignancy and the predicament. Now, I don't feel pity for my brother. I just see his karma unfolding. I feel great compassion. I certainly don't want him to suffer. I realize that I can reduce his suffering by not getting caught in his suffering with him, by being with him at the highest level of consciousness we can meet at, at all times. Therefore, I can help him by working on myself, and all summer long I would go to the Veterans Hospital one day a week and I would sit with him for many hours, just being as conscious as I could be. We would share this space. And all that time he became extraordinarily right here and now, because there wasn't anybody surrounding him that said, "You're nuts," because I don't think he's nuts. I just think he's living on another plane. That plane is a plane, just like this plane is a plane. And he and I would sit around and we'd look at the psychiatrist and we'd say, "Do you think he knows he's God?" And the psychiatrist would say, "They are wondering whether I think I'm God?" A beautiful flip-over predicament we created there, you see. And that reinforcement of my brother's position, he is out of the hospital now, by the way, and he's studying, and it's very strange. He's studying Yoga and he's studying meditation. It's not all pure, by any means. He's perhaps just waiting for the day he can go back to being the Christ again, you know. And maybe he's just cooling it so he won't get locked up. I don't know the level at which he's playing the game.

Compassion without Pity

I have worked for ten years under the model that there was nobody that I couldn't make contact with if I could purify myself enough, you see. That was the model I worked under. And I have dealt with many, many emergency situations when I was a therapist and LSD guide with people calling up in terrible states. And generally what I deal with is I go immediately to the place where I feel compassion for their predicament, but no pity, and I don't get caught in a symbiotic role to the dance they're presenting to me. I center, that's what I do on myself, so that somebody calls up and says, "This is horrible and I'm going to commit suicide." I say, "Well, then don't let me keep you. If you've got to go do that, you do whatever you need to do. But I just want you to know I'm here, if you want to hang out for a while before you commit suicide. Since you're going to do it anyway, you know what you've got to do, but if you'd like to hang out, here we are." And I always am right here. A girl calls me in the middle of the night and she says, "I've taken LSD and my mind is falling apart," and she's crying hysterically. She calls from California to New York. And I say, "Well, who called me?" She says, "Well, I did." I say, "Well, who dialed the number?" She says, "I did." Well, I say, "Would you put whoever it was that dialed the number on, because whoever dialed seven digits plus an area code in the middle of the night to find me, that person I can talk to. You, you're a raving maniac."

That is, I am perfectly convinced that always in another human being there is that place, if I can just cut through to that place, which is my own ability to not get caught in the melodrama each time. Now often it becomes an ego struggle and all I do is center because a person does what he can do.

73

And I never, at any time, get involved. I just do what I do. If the person can make the contact, fine. If he can't, there are often times when custodial care is required for a person, because he is doing work. You see, I'm very far out and I'm somewhat scary from a societal point of view, because I'm not sure I can tell you that two years in a mental hospital isn't much more advantageous in one's growth as a being than four years of a college education. And that maybe six months in prison could be comparable to a post-graduate education in education.

I'm not sure I can look at total-care institutions as other than total-care institutions that do a certain kind of training and provide you with a certain kind of psychological environment. And I do see that there are points in the transformation in beings where they "can't keep it all together." That is, where more is happening to them than they fit, so that they can't keep all the planes together at any one moment. So they get stuck in one plane or another. A schizophrenic goes into one and then flips back into the other, and flips back and forth. Somebody that's totally psychotic stays in another plane. Somebody that is a total anxiety neurotic is afraid to leave this plane. You know, there are all these deep, different gradations.

It seems to me that we must introduce into our society the concept that there are socially sanctioned moratorium centers, there are places where a person can have a total-care environment, where they can go through the changes they need to go through with respect for the fact that they are doing work on themselves. I would say now that a good 40 percent of my friends have been through mental hospitals because they didn't see the world like the psychiatric community saw the world. And I would say that they are now out and that they are some of the highest beings in our culture, and they are functioning optimally and effectively and quite beautifully as human beings. And I think that they did their work often with the help of very hip psychiatrists, and often in spite of the psychiatrist.

I think that many of them just needed that kind of total environmental protection while they did the work. And the psychiatrist needed the security that he was doing something, so he met with the patient so many times and he did his thing. The patient humored him, and then kept doing the work he needed to do on himself. I only guide patients, and I say, "Cool it, baby, so they won't, you know, shoot you up with stuff or shoot your brain full of electric current, or stuff like that. Just cool it enough so that doesn't happen, and then just use it as a moratorium center. It's a groovy ashram. It'll protect you. It's cool."

I visit and I see that prisons and schools are baby-sitting institutions so that we don't glut the labor market. A lot of what is being taught as Western education, is a total, phony hype, as everybody knows. It has nothing to do with anything. It's initiation rites, so you can play ball in the big league park, which has nothing necessarily to do with any great payoff. I think that we are realizing that education is a much more profound matter than the way we've been trivializing it through our schools of education, of which I used to be a professor. I begin to see that we don't learn like rats, primarily, that it is not memory curves based on learning as object. There are other ways of relating to the universe, so that one learns in what would be called Gutherian one-trial learning, if one wants to play science games. I guess that's what I have to say about psychosis. How far out it all is.

Attractions and Dangers of Powers

The Zen masters never get into all these fantastic things that Yogis can do, like go without eating and materialize objects at will and things like that because all those are merely powers. They are the use of powers that exist on various planes between here and where it is you're going. What happens is you get your rational mind and then you can do all these groovy things with it. Well, once you can read other people's minds, you can do even groovier things with it. Once you can do astral travel, there's no end to the groovy things you can do. You always want to do groovy things with them. "I can help mankind with this new power." Well, in fact, every time you do that, it just sticks you in another level of the dance of being stuck still in separateness. You haven't finished the trip. After a while of doing that one, you're going to see that that one is finite, too. It's groovier than the last one was, but it's still finite, and you're going to have to go on beyond that one, too. So that the Zen Buddhists say, "Look, don't stop along the way at all. That's illusion, too. Forget about it. Don't think about it. Don't use it. Don't do it. Don't worry about it."

On the other hand, in other methods that take you through a more stepwise graded process along the way, these powers appear, and the problem is that the game is not to use the power. Most of these stories you hear of high beings using powers are really stories of the powers being manifest, although the high being isn't necessarily using them in an ego sense, the way we would use powers. They're just being used, but he's not getting stuck in them. They are merely cul-de-sacs along the way. All those stories, they're interesting things, and they sure fascinate us as Westerners because they're going to give us all this new power, which we still want because we still think we're separate from it all, and we think we've got to have power. Once you understand that the place you're going to is the transcendence of the experience of separateness, so that you *are* power, see. . . . When Christ says "Had ye but faith, ye could move mountains," he's not putting you on. This is not some lovely metaphor saying it's hard just to lead a good clean life. That isn't what it's about at all. He's just telling you how it is: that were you at a certain level of consciousness you could move a mountain, literally. But the way it happens is very far out. It only happens when you have transcended that in you which is separate from the mountain, so that you are, in fact, the mountain, and then you move. I'm giving it to you straight. You can say it's nutty. I'm just telling you how it is. Later you'll know, if you don't know now. To the extent that you

76

are the mountain that moves, you are also the being that put the mountain there in the first place. He neglected to say that could you move mountains, you probably wouldn't because you put it there in the first place. That's the added part of the thing, which is the final place you go out.

So the Zen Buddhists say, "Just don't attend to all that. It's just going to get you stuck on the way." Other people say, "Well, I need a more gentle method"; and that method gets you caught. Now I am working with a method that is gentle, and yet it always instructs you very carefully: don't use your powers, let them go. I had a few experiences that shook me up, to say the least. I received a letter from my teacher in India, and he said, "After a period of a few months doing the sadhana you're doing, you will be able to read other people's minds." I thought, "Oh, wow, I sure don't want that because that's the last thing a huge ego like me needs, you know. I'll be stuck in that one for the next fifty incarnations, just going around doing good, you know, like 'Let me do good.'" And I'd have these fantasies like, "What'll I do when I can go into other people's minds? I'll go into (at that time it was Lyndon Johnson), I'll become Lyndon Johnson's mind and I'll think loving thoughts toward Mao and I'll become Mao's mind and I'll think loving thoughts toward Lyndon and then I'll become all the members of the United Nations . . . there's no limit to what I can do as a Yogi." Then when I thought it all up, I said, "Well, why didn't the guys do it who are ready?" It gave me pause, like maybe they know something I don't know, you know? Maybe in my zeal to do good I'm going to. . . . I started to see that I was upsetting balances in the universe that would be very destructive if I didn't understand it all. I had to understand it all before I started to play those games. See? So I kept hoping that maybe I'd bypass the whole power trip.

About a year ago I was up at Esalen in Big Sur, and they gave me a house up in the hills where you had to walk up a long walk to get to see me. I was called the Holy Man of Gorda, right? I sat up there, being a Holy Man. It's as good a role as a psychiatrist or a social worker or an educator. It's just another role, you know. And I would sit there every day, and I'd be the holy man, and people would come to be holified or whatever it is you come to see a holy man about, to hang out, mainly and, you know, enjoy the vibes together.

One day there were about forty people sitting around and a man walked in. He was about fifty-five or so, I'd say, and he was a minister. I'd never seen him before, but he sure looked like a minister, but I didn't know that he was a minister. And I started to talk about religion, just because it came into my head to talk about. And then somebody said to me, "Do you have any powers?" And I made the answer I just made to you, "No, I'm happy I don't, because if I did, I have a big ego, and I'd misuse them." And then I looked at this man—he had just arrived and it was late in the afternoon and I sort of wanted to include him into the group in this kind of socially concerned manner and I thought I'd use him as an example. I said, "Could you imagine," and I pointed to this man, "if I could look at you, sir, and I could say, 'You were walking up the hill to get here and you looked down on the ground and you saw what you thought was a jewel and you picked it up and you threw it away.' Could you imagine if I could tell about things like that in your life?" He stood up and turned ashen white. He held onto his chair, and everybody's silent, and he says, "I was walking up the hill," and he said, "I saw this and I picked it up and I thought it was jade and it turned out to be a piece of ginger ale bottle and I threw it away." He sat down, and everybody was silent. And I looked at the picture of my guru and I said, "O.K., baby, cut it out." Because I saw that, you know, that's the worst . . . boy, who needs that? In Yiddish it's called like a *Loch in Kop*, like a hole in the head you need that one, I tell you. That's all you need. That gets you crucified almost immediately.

Nobody ever tells me anything over there. I'm the water boy on the team. I don't know anything about my guru's life at all. I don't know where he came from, how old he is, what he did before. I just know a lot of anecdotes about his recent experiences that people tell me about—you know, what he did, he did this, and he did that. There was only one picture of him when he was young, and what he looked like was a totally zonked-out Sunset Strip hippie, with long hair and beard and he looks like he's sitting in Ben Frank's in Los Angeles, you know, just looking off into space and he's totally zonked out of his head. Somebody came along in the jungle and took this picture of him, and whatever he was experiencing at that point was very far out. I don't know any more than that.

NEED FOR A GURU

The question of whether you need a guru: there are stages in your development where you need a guru. However, you've got to understand what a guru is. A guru is not a teacher. The relation between the guru and chela is not interpersonal, it's intrapersonal. That is, that element of my guru which is a little old man in a blanket over in India is just a little old man in a blanket over in India. He knows everything in my head. He is everything in my head, and he's as much here as he is there. If he isn't as much here as he is there, he's a hype, and I shouldn't be thinking of him as a guru, anyway. So therefore the whole idea that I would go anywhere to see the guru must obviously be a fallacy. Right? That's the first part of it. So then I realize that each person finds his guru as soon as he's ready to find his guru. That is, as soon as your head is open enough, he's available to you, because there's only one of them, in the purest sense, since it's not connected with ego in that sense, right? So "I'm looking for a guru" is obviously a trip like any other trip. We'll call it *Looking for the Guru*, which is the thing you do before you despair of finding the guru, which is the prerequisite to opening your head to finding the guru. Despair is the necessary prerequisite for the next degree of consciousness. That's absolutely a prerequisite.

So a lot of what we see in our society as a malaise that we call deep despair and depression is in fact this consciousness-transformation that's occurring, this absolutely necessary pre-requisite before we can start to hear the next level, which is a very deep despair and a depression about everything we have going. Rather than teaching each other to adapt to what we have, it would be better to honor the despair and allow a person to be in that despair until he comes through it, hopefully coming through it in a more evolved fashion, if he's got support for it.

As far as teachers are concerned, a teacher is wherever you are when you're ready for that teacher. That is, if you hear enough to ask the question, "How am I going to get on with my work?" and you say, "Well, what I ought to do is calm my mind down," then you'd say, "Well, how do I calm my mind down?" Now asking that question sensitizes you to see a lot of beings around you who have been busy calming their minds down, or teaching people how to calm their minds down, that until then you've passed by and never even noticed existed, because you were so busy thinking of them as kooks, nuts, cranks, or people that do those things; but they're nice guys, anyway. Suddenly that's the thing about them that you want to know, you see. And so you begin to find out that your teachers are often people who have been right around you. They're called *Upa Gurus*, as opposed to *Sat Guru*. The Sat Guru is somebody who beckons from beyond. He's somebody who's all finished. The Upa Guru is anybody or anything along the way that points the path that helps you along a little way. So that even your enemies often are your Upa Gurus because they wake you up to a place you're not, which helps you get free of that place, which helps you get on with it. So you learn to honor everybody you meet as your teacher when you see that there is nothing else you can do but be conscious, for the good of yourself and all your fellow men, and to bring you closer to the place you're trying most to get to by all the other means you thought you were working on. You work on your own consciousness, and the way to do that is to see the teaching that is in everything in the universe—about where you're not conscious or where you're asleep.

You begin to see that everything in your universe becomes your teacher.

So your teacher is everywhere. Your guru is waiting for you to be ready for him. That's the model you can work on. So you don't have to rush to India because it's always right where you are. There are beings who can get as high as any enlightened being ever got, sitting in the middle of Topeka, Kansas, or in the middle of New York, or in the middle of anywhere. It depends on your readiness, and that has to do with your karma or your readiness to get on with it.

GNOSTIC INTERMEDIARY

Why am I going back? At the level I function at, I'm almost going back because I'm going back. I wouldn't say I have any profound model of why I'm going back. I'm going back because my karmic attachments to that whole scene aren't done yet. I also see that my role, my thing, in the water-flowing-downstream, dispassionate, Taoist sense is that I am a Western teacher and that all of the experiences I had as a middle-class person and as a psychedelicist and as a social scientist and a cellist and a pilot and all those things are all part of my preparation to be able to teach what I have to teach. And I see that part of my role is that of a gnostic intermediary, that is, to bring metaphors from one system into another system. That seems to be my thing. It's done without attachment, in that I'm doing it because I'm doing it because I'm doing it because I'm doing it. That is, I do this and I do this and I do this, and there are tapes being made, and those tapes are going to be listened to by thousands and thousands of people, because they just pour around the country now and everything I've had to say up until now, as a teacher, is said. I've done what I have to do. Now I'm free to go the next round inward. I can go into a cabin in New Hampshire or in a cabin in Topeka, or just sit down and meditate and get on with it, but I also can go and pick up more metaphors as a teacher along the way, which is part of my teaching.

81

I don't have a model. All I can see is that I am a teacher and as a teacher you collect more. You see, the peculiar predicament I'm in is that I go back to the feet of this little old man in a blanket and I'm in the relation to the guru of chela. It's his trip, not mine any more. I am in the role of service. I am now living out—and I now understand in the most profound sense—what it means to say, "Not mine, but Thy will." So I'm just doing the trip. I'm not writing the script at the moment. When I get back, he may say, "You've finished your work," and touch me, and I turn into a butterfly, I don't know. Or I may go back and he kicks me and says, "I don't know who you are: Go back to America." I can't write the script. I don't know. And that is very difficult for our Western culture, where you usually have a model of what you're going to do and you're collecting this for that and you're living in time. I'm not living in time, that way.

The Fourth, Fifth, Sixth, and Seventh Chakras

As I said earlier, there are seven chakras or focal points and the transition from the third to the fourth is the first one into the transcendent state. It's the first one into the state of compassion, that is, where one experiences the shifts over figure-ground relationship so that one sees that you and I are human beings behind not only blue-suitness or dark-suitness and white-shirtness but also behind personalities and ages and bodies, and there is a place where—although we still see each other as separate—we are experiencing a feeling of a unitive nature with one another. That is another level of consciousness, where that unitive nature is *real*, rather than intellectually known. It's a real plane. And that compassion is the compassion that what is happening to you is happening to me, because in that place you and I are a unitive being. We're just two different manifestations of that one consciousness. That's already fourth chakra.

The fifth chakra is where you turn back inward, and rather than seeing the outward manifestations, you start to go deeper within or deeper up, as you might call it, and become pre-occupied with higher planes of light or energy or form of it all, which are more and more subtle states of differences and similarities. It's as if we come into the place where we are energy or where we are cellular formations. It's sort of different planes of perceptual organization of the universe. You could put it that way, what these planes are about.

The sixth chakra is very comparable to what's called the causal plane, which is a place where one has broken sufficient attachments to any one perspective, so that you can stand back sufficiently far to gain what could be called cosmic perspective, to begin to see the most basic laws of the universe in operation everywhere in the universe. It's very much what the Egyptians were concerned with. It's what Plato's pure ideas are primarily about. That is sixth chakra. It's what we call wisdom. It's the wisdom of the ages, of these laws, these very simple laws. It could also be called the Godhead in a religious formulation of the first thought forms, the thought out of which all the rest is manifestation. At that place you are in the realm of pure ideas. That is, if you are in the sixth chakra, you have in a sense left the gross body. You are no longer identified with this body, nor are you identified with your personality, even, which is a more subtle plane. You are only identified with the ideas, all the rest is but manifestation, coming outward in planes of grossness.

The seventh chakra, the top chakra, is the chakra where you merge back into the oceanic, into the one, totally. If you would look, for example, at the cyclic process of ocean mist rising off ocean, forming clouds, clouds have raindrops, raindrops fall into ocean, ocean is made up of raindrops, but it's ocean, and it's ocean in the sense of oneness. Each raindrop does not retain its individuality as a raindrop any longer. And you can see this is merely process. The seventh chakra is the ocean. It's where it all goes back into the one. It's even behind all the laws and ideas.

Now, when one is climbing this ladder, at each new level

there is a new way in which you can receive energy or transmute energy in the universe. You can work with different kinds of energy when you are localized at each chakra, than you could before. You eat different foods, you can work with light, with love, and so on—different ways. Also, you see the universe in different ways and therefore your actions or responses start— your habits of thinking about it all, and thus your responses— start to change with each new level as well. At each level you are inclined to get stuck in that level. You have to, at each level, go beyond that one, too. What is usually the case for most of us who are doing this work is that we are very unevenly distributed in our energy over the different chakras or planes. That is, there is a certain part of me that is open in the fifth chakra. There is a certain degree to which I am starting to be opened in the sixth chakra. There is a way in which I am opened in the fourth chakra, very deeply opened in the fourth chakra. I still have much energy attached to the second chakra, sexual chakra, and the third chakra, in terms of power and so on. Now the process is to slowly "convert *Bindu* to *Ogis*," or transmute energy, or move it up into these higher and higher chakras, because every higher chakra is a more total organization of the entire universe in a more and more cosmic way of perceiving it and understanding and living with it all, which means a higher level of functioning, if you will.

The job is to take energy from a lower center and move it to a higher center. This becomes the work. What I can do is, through various techniques, I can center primarily on the fourth chakra and then when something happens that is in a lower chakra, I can convert it to that fourth chakra. So that if I am centered in the fourth chakra, and a beautiful girl comes along and I experience lust or arousal in the terms of subject-object, which would be a second-chakra relationship, I can at the same moment see that she is God and I am God and we are in the manifestations of male and female. This is an eternal drama that has been lived out, and I can in that process make contact with that place in her which is behind woman-ness and in

84

me behind man-ness. Then we will either do out the dance or not, depending on what a lot of conditions are, but we are no longer stuck in that place of lust. So when the Bible says, "Thou shalt not lust," it's really speaking about, "Thou shalt not get stuck at the second chakra," is one way of saying that same thing.

Now I would say that my own state and that of most of us in the West who are working is quite uneven, and spread over most states. I have, through psychedelics originally, and more recently through pranayam, gotten into sixth and seventh chakra states. In psychedelics I would stay many hours in what would be called *Nirvikalpa Samadhi*, a very very high form of samadhi, a completely formless void. Now there are many reasons for coming back from that place into lower chakras, or lower ways of organizing the universe. You can come back because of "uncooked seeds," that is, because there is still some energy or libido cathected at those lower centers. However, in order to fulfill the entire journey you begin to understand what the Bodhisattva role is in Buddhism: that is, that even getting to the seventh plane, you can get stuck at that place, too. And if you are at that plane, to the negation of the other planes, you are still not finished. You are attached to the void, it's called. The final place you end up coming to is where you complete the cycle. And you come back into every plane and you live consciously at every plane, because every plane is another truth. It's another level of truth. And you live in a Bodhisattva role, which means living in this world of illusion at the same time that you are not in the world of illusion, because you are fully conscious at the seventh chakra also. That is, you are conscious right across the planes simultaneously.

OPTIMUM BEING

The job finally is not just to keep moving it up but to move it up until you are free of each one, including the last one, so that you are at all of them, all the time. You are the optimum being at every level. That must seem to be what it's about. I can't walk out on the illusion, if you're stuck in the illusion, since you are part of me. So if you're stuck, I'm stuck. So, where can I go? I can't go out and finish my own trip at your expense, since who ends up being caught in that but us. And I'm part of us. I've already seen that in the fourth chakra, you see. A person can't really go on his own trip all by himself and forget it.

Now there are some beings whose work at these different planes is reasonably finished—this has something to do with karma—and therefore they are at the point where they end up in the seventh chakra. There are some sadhus in India, for example, who go into the seventh chakra and don't come back—not because they are stuck, but because their work is done, in that sense. They have divested all of their gross body and subtle personality; they have divested any energy from it. The rule of the game under these conditions is that after twenty-one days their body falls apart, because there is no motivating principle or thought, of which it is a manifestation, maintaining it any longer. As long as you want to have hallucinations, you've got to have somebody thinking the hallucination. When there's nobody around thinking it, the hallucination falls away, including the body, at that point. That only happens under a few conditions.

Now we have interesting models in history to work with because we have not only a Buddha, who goes all the way through and ends in the seventh plane, which is the Buddha state, and then comes back into the world and plays out the role form that he is as a Bodhisattva, meaning he stays on this plane at the same time that he is finished with all planes. We have also the model of a Christ, whom I can comfortably deal with as a being who doesn't come up through the ranks, so to speak, but is a direct manifestation of mind into matter, in order to play out a certain part. Now this is a different kind of storyline for us to work with, because it is as if a sixth or seventh chakra being takes a gross body manifestation for a certain function in the total drama of Man's coming out of the illusion. See, he's playing his part in it in that way, because there is rhyme and reason and law and order at each of these planes of existence. There are beings that are existing at these planes of existence, because only at the planes below the fourth chakra do you need to maintain a body. There are beings that do exist who have personalities and all kinds of individual differences, but they are not manifested in bodily form. They are not manifest on this particular frequency that you and I can pick up through our senses and our thinking minds. This does not refute their existence. It merely means our instruments at this moment, in this way of doing it, can't know them, because we don't know how to measure them. We can sometimes meet them, and I can meet them when I will leave this particular plane, as if I'm tuning my television receiver, which turns out to be tuning into various nerves or what are called in the Sanskrit *nadis*, or as if they are like electrically finer receivers in my body. There is, for example, a type of Yoga that I work with called *Nad Yoga*, which is the Yoga of Inner Sound. That is, I put in ear plugs and I listen. You can hear, for example, you might hear the ocean roar or crickets or the sound of a crowd in a railroad terminal or flutes . . . a variety of sounds. They are organized sounds.

What you are doing is you are almost tuning into a different set of nerves that are functioning in your body. You're hearing your own nerves function, in a way. And when you do this, each of these nerves is also connected with one of these chakras or one of these levels. So that what you do is, whatever sound you hear inside, instead of just listening to it, you allow yourself to merge with that sound and then when you are one with that sound—from that vantage point you hear the next sound. Right? You change your stepping position. It's like you climb steps by sound. You use sounds as your stepping points. You can't jump two steps, you go up one step, and then from that place you hear the next inner sound. This is a very high form of yoga. It's focusing on sound rather than on visual fields. It's the one-pointedness of sound. Well, now each of those sounds is connected with another astral plane and as you work with these sounds you see they're connected with colors, vibrations, with hallucinations or different kinds of realities that you start to see. There are sounds connected with each of them. And so you can imagine that you can work with these inner sounds as a way of leading yourself into these other states of consciousness.

Most of the time, I am functioning in an interesting place, I guess—it sort of seems interesting from where I'm sitting—because it almost seems most of the time as if I am sitting in a completely calm, centered place where nothing whatsoever is happening, or could ever happen. And yet, all of this is happening. But there is some way in which I have broken my identification with this happening. It is very much of a fourth-chakra journey in the sense that what I feel, the emotions I feel, are waves of compassion and love for all my being. I mean, I can get on a bus and by the time I get off I feel like I have met my most intimate family that I've known all my life. And we're all in love with one another. That's the type of experience I'm having with the world around me. It's scary because of the degree of openness that it entails. There's got to be an awareness that you are not vulnerable on the separateness level before you can let yourself live in that place. And I see life processes going on, but I don't feel identified with them like I used to. So now what I am doing is, I am trying to cook the seeds of my third chakra by playing out some of these games, because this game, for example, involves power. It involves fame. It involves a number of third-chakra concerns that I used to be preoccupied with getting in the old days, coming up from the tradition I came out of. But now every time I get one of those, I see how it is a liability in my journey, you see. So I can hand it back, right? I can realize that the highest response I can get from an audience now is where they see that what I've been talking about is inside themselves, and that I was just a vehicle for them to hear, and I'm no great shakes, you see. The minute I end up with people saying, "Oh, you're something and I'm not," I know I'm too impure. I'm still doing it in the third chakra, you see. I'm still doing it in a way for me to grab the power, right? And I've got to be able to give up the power all the time. Otherwise my message is not pure. So that this is a market-place journey for me to try to cook my third chakra seeds, if you would like a technical description of what I think I'm doing.

TRANSMUTATION OF ENERGY

If I am at one point, when something happens in my field, my environmental field, that's negative, what I say is, "That brings me down," meaning it caught me in its model of how it all is. When I am able to transmute energy, I can take that energy that was connected with that act itself and I can move it up my chakras and get high from it. Right? Not only can I get high from it, but I can give back a place which frees the other person from it as well. That is, if you come up to me and go "R-r-r-r-r" I can be busy going "R-r-r-r," see, or I can see you going "R-r-r-r" and say, "Yes, and that too is life and here we are and that's the way it is." And then I can look at you and be with you in a certain way where I took all that energy you fed in and it just pulled it up my spine and here we are in this new higher place together which then frees you from the place you were stuck in before as well. Now, for example, every night for three weeks I gave *darshan* in New York City in a sculpture studio for about two hundred people and more people kept coming and they kept coming back and more kept coming every night and it was just like a curve, a geometric curve, and just more and more we were getting higher and higher together. But the place was next door to a fire house and usually you could count on the fact that at least once or twice a night the fire engines would be called out. And we might be in the middle of chanting a love song to God, you know, in this very intimate sound and suddenly "R-r-r-r-r-r" and you'd look out into the audience and everybody was going through that pained "Oh, they've loused it up and we've lost our moment." And I looked at that and I thought, "Wow, isn't that far out?" Here all these high beings are being brought down by a fire engine. What I do is, I see the fire engine is merely free energy the city of New York is giving us if we know how to use it, and I'm getting stoned out of my head, getting way up into these higher chakras off the fire engine. And I'm saying, instead of seeing life as full of impediments to doing what your pre-run tape says you're supposed to do, see all of it as part of the here and now moment. There's the fire engine and that's the way it is. You're only bugged with it if you're still living a moment ago where you were busy not having the fire engine. At the moment, here's the fire engine. If you can live in the here and now, you should say, "Wow, here's the fire engine." Then you're in a new state. That's transmuting that energy. In other words, it's getting high off of it.

Now you can take almost any experience that you will have at the lower level and you can, by re-perceiving it in a certain way, just bring it up to another level and get more energy off it. Tantra means using the senses to go beyond the senses. Sexual tantra, which is using a partner, a sexual partner, as a vehicle to transcend through . . . often involves that I can sit down with a desirable sexual object, whoever that may be, to put it in a rather impersonal sense, and focus between the eyes with that person and enter into a place where I can see that which is desirable in the person, they can see that which is desirable in me. We can both see we are desiring each other but instead of rushing immediately into the melodrama that the desire leads to, we stay in that place. We look and we see that there we are, being beings who see those desire trips. Then it starts to change and we see that we are also something else and we're also something else and for many of us if I look into anybody's eyes for more than about ten seconds, their face starts to change and I start to see all beings in every being. I see all faces because in a way we are all beings. There's an element of everything in us. That's what I'm sure Jung was referring to at one point about collective unconscious.

So that when you can take the energy that is aroused through

the lust that you experienced through the desire for the partner, and take that energy and stay with it instead of running
that game through, you just keep bringing the energy into a
higher place. You see, you're using that energy to get higher
and higher and higher and higher. You see how that's working?
And so pretty soon you've taken that energy formed by the
relation between the polar opposites, which is this fantastic
force or *Shakti*, as it's called in the Hindu system, and you've
used that energy to bring yourself into higher states of consciousness. That's why marriages in India are arranged by the
astrologer and they are specifically designed to become conscious
through. They aren't models that we in the West are concerned
with. We marry for different reasons than they marry because
we are not living in the spirit. We're living in the world of
materiality and we respond to our passions that way. We feel if
we're not responding, then we're getting gypped. Well, actually
all we're doing is we're making second and third chakra contracts. And once you've started to be in the fourth chakra you
start to re-negotiate the contracts that can be re-negotiated and
live out honorably the ones that must be lived out at the other
levels. But most of them you convert, you transmute. So that if
a parent gets higher, the relation with his child gets higher. If a
husband gets higher, his wife gets higher with him. That's part
of that dance.

CENTERING

Can you get high off somebody else's low, or do you get
high even though somebody else is low? Yeah, you see, to the
extent that you have a center independent of their consciousness, you can then take whatever energy anybody or anything
feeds you and bring it to that center and get higher off it. But
I would point out that I'm sure many patients cure their
psychiatrists in the sense that they do the work that gets them
into a form of consciousness that frees the psychiatrist from
the predicament he was stuck in in "doing good," which is a
beautiful place and also a horrible place, depending on how

stuck you are in it. And so, a relationship is as high as the highest consciousness, even though it may only be a contact high. It is true, that if you come up and have any relationship to me, come on to me in any way, if I can stay centered, it takes two of us to do a dance, whatever it is. If you're angry, I've got to be angry back or something. I've got to be something back for you to be able to maintain that dance. It's very hard to maintain it in an environment where there's no support for it at all, see? And so all I can do is center so much that all you get back from me is a mirror of who you are and you see exactly where you're at. And at the same moment my mirror is in no way pejorative. As long as I have a value that where I'm at is better than where you're at, then I'm coming on to you in the most subtle way saying, "Look how conscious I am, and look how centered I am," see? You can't come on. That's impure. You can only be where you are and each person gets what he needs to get. I can't do anything to, for, or about you, all I can do is be what I be. Through your interaction with me, you may or may not change, see? And I teach because I teach because I teach. And I therapize because I therapize because I therapize. I don't therapize to save souls. And I don't teach because I'm concerned about your well-being although in the process something good may happen to you. Because it will create new problems for me. But at the ego level, I sure hope so.

Distinctions Between English and Sanskrit

Let me for a moment deal with that distinction between English and Sanskrit. Now when Sanskrit was evolved as a letter language of fifty-four symbols, I guess, or fifty—I think it's fifty—it was evolved by beings who saw each of these symbols connected with different relations of consciousness. Patterns of symbols put together were put together in order to, when you worked with them, take you to that level of consciousness. English has all the sounds in it, but it was not designed with that kind of level of consciousness in the designation of the way in which the sequences work together. There is a mantra that was set up by a Tibetan lama to understand the West. It's a very interesting one, in Sanskrit, which says, in effect, *Please, please, sorry, thank you.* All you say over and over again is *Please, please, sorry, thank you, Please, please, sorry, thank you.* And because it has all those excess meanings, all the over-meanings of social roles that we work with in the immense amount of time we say "Please," "Sorry," and "Thank you," it as a mantra takes you through many, many trips. But the highest level of taking you into a vibrational space it doesn't do, because it wasn't designed with that degree, that level of performance, in itself.

One-Pointedness of Mind

If I had my "druthers" in the field of education at the moment. . . . You know, the last educational experiment I ever did, which was before I got thrown out of Harvard, was I introduced karate into the Lexington school system. And I did it not as karate but as a technique of Eastern exercise. It was a little dishonest in the sense that I brought my karate masters in, and they showed all the junior high school kids, so everybody volunteered because they all wanted to learn to break boards. And it wasn't for that reason at all. That was their motive for doing it but I knew that in order to do it optimally, they would have to develop one-pointedness, see? In other words, they were competing against their own inner struggle. They had to bring their mind to one-pointedness to be able to do this and in the process they would develop this extraordinary discipline of the mind which I felt would transfer into all of the other parts of their life. So I was trying to use the physical education program—instead of developing more ego trips through competitive sports—to try to develop a discipline of mind which I felt would transfer because it seems to me that teaching one-pointedness of mind is a very, very important tool or vehicle for using the rational mind and for work on oneself. And therefore I think I would probably start with very, very early schooling in terms of meditation and so on.

I learned from my teacher in India something very profound. I was a professor of education and I had studied techniques of teaching. I don't think I had ever seen as pure a case as he showed me, that in all the time he taught me I was never under the impression that he was teaching me anything, because he was teaching me from inside myself. And he was doing that from being a wise man and then turning off the model that he was teaching me anything. He became so open that he heard where I was. Then, working from within my framework, he evolved. Whatever came out of him was my framework moving toward the wisdom that he "was." That is, one of the things I would do if I were going to teach a child, I would as quickly as possible get out of any model that I was going to teach this child. That is, by hanging out with this child and saying, "O.K., now what?" Because I am now under the model that the child already knows everything and my job on myself is to thin the veils that keep me from knowing it all, and to not contribute to increasing the veils that keep him from knowing it all, right? To help him thin his veils. So that, what I would be inclined to do, I think, is to sit with a group of people and say, "Let us start from exactly where we are at. All truth is in everything. There is no pre-programmed model in my head that is that vital including any books, any subjects, because I'm now awed by an interesting phenomenon that I've begun to see."

As some of these young teenagers finish their drop-outs from school and their moratorium and their anti-energies, and start to be open in a turned-on way, I see that they can absorb fields of knowledge almost as fast as they can hear it fed in because they are learning it out of a very positive thing. They're ready to hear it and they want to grab it. They learn it almost in "one-trial" learning. They don't learn it with that kind of resistance of subject-object where somebody's implanting it in them before they're ready to know it. So that I guess timing, readiness to learn, becomes a very critical matter and I think I'm willing to handle a lot more tension of "lack of closure" of early noneducation in the formal sense. Rather than getting kindergarten and prekindergarten kids to read earlier and earlier and earlier, running our programs through kids earlier and earlier and earlier, I think I would be inclined to surround children with as high a consciousness as I could find. That is, I think I would first of all institute a program for teachers to work on themselves. That's the first thing I would do. Then I would put them in an environment with these kids where whatever the vehicle was, the teacher saw that as merely a vehicle for us to become conscious together, rather than getting the teacher caught in any other achievement model, such as, "I've got to get a 'pay-off' from these kids in terms of their external performance." That means I'm willing to maintain a certain tension level of lack of performance in these kids for quite a while. I'll play for the long shot that they will open to the universe, which is within them, in a way that will allow them to tune in on stuff much faster than if they learn it in a linear input fashion, in the way that I've been programming it in traditionally. I begin to see that the educator educates himself and then he hangs out with the child and the child gets free of the things that are keeping him from educating himself because, in effect, we only do it to ourselves. That's the model I understand now. We don't do it to each other. We only do it to ourselves. All you can do is provide an environment where the kid can do it to himself. I guess I would be inclined to realize that a classroom is as high as the highest being in the room. And sometimes that's the teacher and sometimes it isn't. Sometimes it's a kid. It is not true that kids are little Buddhas. Everybody's a Buddha, but a kid is deepest in the illusion, in a way, because he had to be born into the illusion or he wouldn't have been born this birth and

95

here he is now and he's in the illusion. Now the question is how long is he going to stay in it? And he's going to stay in it as long as he's got to stay in it, but also as long as people around him are sucking him into it, which is dependent on the extent that they're stuck in it. So all you can do for a child is, really, not be stuck in the illusion yourself. And then that frees the child and the minute he's free he'll pick up everything he needs.

If I need to repair a car, I can damn well figure out how to repair cars. And there's nothing that makes me learn how to repair a car faster than when my car's broken, I'll tell you. I could study theories of carburation until hell freezes over and it would pass through me like Chinese food, but when I need to fix the carburetor I read that manual and boy it really has relevance because I want to know how to fix the carburetor. And there is something about functional knowledge. When the kid has an itch, then he scratches it and until then it's only fun and games in our head. And the whole history of knowledge is as a drop in the bucket compared with wisdom. We're trying to preserve something and what we're doing is preserving at the cost of something much, much higher than is what we really want. We would like to train for wisdom, not knowledge. And what we're training for is knowledge, because we can measure it. But knowledge is not convertible, necessarily, into human happiness or well-being. Wisdom is, because wisdom is learning how to live with the Tao, to live in harmony with the world at the moment it is. Wisdom is a totally adaptive thing, but knowledge isn't. Knowledge is not necessarily adaptive. But if you're a wise being, whatever is, is. You deal with what is. You teach a child methods of how to be conscious, how to use the tool of his mind as an exquisite, analytic device. You teach methods of absorbing knowledge. You don't teach knowledge per se. That's one of the major things. And I think we're moving toward that in elementary education anyway. I think we start to respect each human being's method of evolving and we allow for much wider degrees of freedom in terms of each person's journey. We present him with models of consciousness, not models of external achievement.

TEACHERS AS CONVEYORS OF THE UNIVERSE

I used to work for an outfit called SMSG, the School Mathematics Study Group, which puts experimental mathematics education in public schools. I was their tame psychologist and I would do computer programs and run their data through and design all their assessment projects to find out whether it did any good. I found out this very far-out thing, that most of the women generalist education teachers in the elementary schools were like typhoid carriers of the attitudes toward mathematics because they themselves couldn't count, you know, and they got all up-tight about it. They felt they had to teach it, so they would teach it but they would say, "All right, you've had a good time out at recess, now you can sit down and do your arithmetic," because their attitude toward it was so negative that they inculcated these attitudes. And I began to see that just as a parent is the conveyor of the universe, so each of these teachers are. And the earlier you can help the person out of the illusion, the better off you are. The earlier you can do it the better you help the education system. Your hope is that so many high beings are coming in as freshman that they may help the system save itself, at this point, from total extinction because they're bringing more and more of this stuff to the college campus. I sound horribly radical and all that but I'm not really throwing out the baby with the bath because I see that all of what man has developed in his knowledge and his technology and his humanities and his art forms and so on is living in the present. It's all here right now. There is no chance that it's going to fall away if it has a meaningful human function at this moment. If we are only carrying it on out of guilt, forget it. But if it has a function we'll find it. And we, in a sense, have to re-do the run, over again. Just like ontogeny recapitulates philogeny, so each person's journey into consciousness recapitulates all of man's journey into consciousness. He has to re-find the need

97

to absorb music and art and history and literature. You can't lay it on him because you know it's important. He's got to be ready to hear it. And so that readiness is such a critical issue and that's why these early experiments with preschool and nursery and elementary school are very open environments, allowing the child to listen . . . learn to listen. And that's why these meditation exercises are designed specifically to allow him to hear rather than to get so caught in ego. I think competition and ego-enhancement is one of the things that's got to go. A lot of it, it's really got to go; the competitive models we're using in evaluation and in achievement. We have a model that if we don't achieve, if we don't give an achievement incentive, the whole system will fall down.

I was a worker in the field of achievement motivation and the game was how to get people to want to achieve more. And now I begin to see that when you take all the pressures off, a person says, "Well, if there's no reason to achieve, I won't do anything." And I say, "O.K. Don't do anything. Now what?" He says, "I'm just going to sit in bed." "O.K. That's doing something. You're going to sit in bed. Now what?" "Well, I'm kind of bored sitting in bed." "O.K. Now what are you going to do?" It's as if once we finish with all our fears that it's all going to be chaos, after the moratorium, what a person does is he starts to build a life because he's in a human birth and he's got to make it beautiful and meaningful and rich and stimulating and aesthetically fulfilling. All that stuff happens all over again. But he does it now because he really wants to do it.

Once we finish drafting everybody who doesn't go to college, we're going to find that thousands of these kids are going to drop out of college. Instead of seeing this as a horrible thing, we damned well better start seeing it as a very productive thing and start to respect the journey these kids are on, because they are not rejecting all of our traditions, they're merely rejecting the fraudulence with which we are living out our traditions. When I went to college I went with a lot of veterans and I came right out of high school. And the veterans were there and they were asking entirely different kinds of questions of their education than I was because they had dealt with life and death and, man, they wanted it to mean something to them. I was perfectly delighted to just go through this little mechanical game of being a student which had no more meaning than being a good student. When I taught at Harvard and Stanford and Cal . . . clearly the highest experience was teaching at Cal, because these were city kids who were living in the world and they had to go earn the bread in a gas station to come to college and they wanted to know what the hell does this child psychology have to do with bringing up their kids? They didn't want to sit around and play a lot of high abstract games. At Harvard everybody was delighted to play games. We'll just play games. It doesn't have anything to do with anything. We'll just play games and enjoy the game.

Now you can say, "Well there is a lot of productivity out of that pure, free, untrammeled game-playing." And I can enjoy that as a research strategy. I don't enjoy it as a process of education. I don't see it as a process of education.

In India when people meet and part, instead of saying hello or goodbye, they say something to each other . . . which reminds us of who we are. They say, "I honor the Atman within you, I honor the light which is within you," meaning, I look into you for that place where we are, behind all of our individual differences. And the word they use is *Namasta*. Na-ma-sta. It means "I honor the light within you." So may I close by saying to all of you, Namasta.

three

Since my training was similar to that of some of you, and certainly ten or fifteen years ago I might well have been found in an installation such as this, it might be useful to share with you why I am at the moment sitting cross-legged with a name like Ram Dass and pursuing the path that I am presently pursuing, rather than remaining within academia or within the traditional research structures. I just returned in the spring from my second visit to India, and why I go there will become apparent, I think, shortly.

I have in India a teacher. It's more than a teacher as I'll explain in a little while. When I went back to India I went back to go to him for further teaching. He is what's known as a Jungle Sadhu. That is, he has lived many years in the jungle. He's a very simple man and he moves around from village to village. He has a loin cloth and a blanket, and many devotees of different cities build temples, such as this place is, in a way, in hopes that he will come and that he will stay there; but he comes and he drops by and then he disappears again. Or he goes off in the night somewhere. So it's very hard to find him, because in India—well, to characterize the feeling of India— those of you in the audience that have been living in the United States for many years may recall the time when you would place a telephone call, and they would say that it would take about three or four hours to get through to, say, Chicago, and then when you would get it, it would be "Hello, hello, can you hear me?" It's that kind of thing, and it's static and crossed telephone messages, and most of the communications between villages are by telegraph or by mail because the telephones are so absurd. I mean they are really almost out of the question, and each village is in a sense quite isolated, so to find somebody who is moving around is not easy. You just hear by word of mouth that he was here, or you heard somebody's brother-in-law just came in from so and so and told you that he might be there. I have found from experience with this man that if he wants me, he'll find me, and it's best for me not to try to figure out where he is, since he is better at the game than I am.

When I came to India this last time, I went to his usual haunts and he wasn't there. So I went to a place called Bodh Gaya, which is where Buddha received enlightenment. I went into a Burmese Ashram where they were training in Southern Buddhist meditation. I pursued this meditation with a number of other Westerners, about 100 other Westerners, for about two months; a very isolated little village. It could have gone on and on, a continuous thing, but at the end of two months I felt that I had gotten what I could get at that time from that particular technique. Although I felt I wanted to go deeper, I couldn't at that moment, and I had been invited informally by a very eminent swami to come to Delhi for a holy festival. Delhi is about 250–300 miles away. So, sort of at the last minute, a few days earlier, I decided I would go.

When a number of these people heard that I was going and that there was a possibility of this festival in Delhi, they all decided, many of them, that they would like to go. So it turned out that there were maybe about thirty-four of us that wanted to go to Delhi. It also happened that one of the girls had come from London to India aboard one of these tour buses that you pay so many pounds and you go to Delhi by bus, or Afghanistan or so. The bus driver was hanging around in India waiting for a return tour to take back to England, and he sort of was a little soft on this girl, and he thought it would be kind of nice to hang out with us. And he had this huge big bus. So about two days before, she received a letter asking could he come and be with us. He was in a nearby city, and we sent him a telegram saying, "If you want to meet us, we will all go with you to Delhi," and suddenly thirty-four of us just get on his bus and go to Delhi. And the route goes through a city called Allahabad, which is a very old city.

Now Allahabad has a very special significance in the spiritual world of India, because it is where certain very holy rivers meet, and it's the scene of what is called the Khumba Mela which is the gathering of holy beings from around India. They come to the confluence of these rivers at a certain time in relation to the moon and so on at a certain time each year. Every twelve years is a major festival, and each year there is a small one. We were going through there about a week after it was over, I guess. One of the boys, Danny Goleman, who is also a psychologist, had previously left the meditation course and gone to see the Khumba Mela when it was held, and he had come back and told us how beautiful it was. As we were heading toward Delhi—it was now late in the afternoon—he said, "I'd love to have you all see where the Mela was held." I was sort of in command, and I said, "Well, it's kind of late in the day, and really we have a small child here, and we're all a little tired and we have a long trip. Why don't we pass it up this time? After all, the Mela is all over. We're just going to see an empty place, you know." And Danny said, "Yes, but the vibrations will be very beautiful." Well, you know vibrations are very ephemeral, and you may get them and you may not. It's just an empty fairground from one way of looking—depending on how tired you are. So, I said, no, I didn't think we would do that. He said, "O.K." He went back and sat down. I was sitting up with the bus driver. And I thought, Well, you know, I'm being pretty square about all this. After all, you've just got to drive off the road and it's maybe fifteen minutes to get to this fairground and this place, and we could go and we could spend maybe fifteen-twenty minutes and watch the sunset and then go on. That would be nice. And I reflected about the pros and cons and whether we would get to a hotel in time for the night, and when the food would be available, and I was thinking all these thoughts. Finally I said, "All right, we'll go," and I said to the driver, "Right up here is the junction, and you turn right here." It was a bumpy road, and I thought, "Gee, I don't know whether I made the right decision, but . . ." We come down this long hill to this huge ground, which is now empty. It's like a carnival ground after the carnival has left. So there is sort of papers blowing in the wind. It was very deserted and there were the rivers in the distance. And Danny said, "You know those little medallions I bought at the Mela. I bought them from a stand right over there, so why don't we just park right over there? That's a nice place, and we'll just sit there for a few minutes." So we pulled the bus over to park, and just as we're parking one of the boys looks and he yells. "There's Maharaj-ji!" which is the name of my guru, or teacher.

Maharaj-ji walks by the bus, and he has with him another man, and he stops at the end of the bus—there are no other human beings around, by the way—and he says, "Well, they've come," to the other man. We got out and we rush to him and we fall at his feet, and he says, "Come, follow me." We follow in the bus behind this rickshaw and we go to this house. It's around 5:30 or 6 at night, and we walk into the house where food has been prepared since morning for thirty-four people, and where lodgings have been arranged for thirty-four people for the night. Now, all I ask you at the beginning, at the outset, is who was it that thought he was sitting in the bus deciding whether he would go to those grounds or not? This is the predicament I'm faced with, being around this man. Who do I think I am? What do I really think the game is? My confrontation with a being such as this man is forcing me—previously trained as a psychologist—to confront what *is* human decision-making? What is ego, what is personality, what is choice? What is free will? What is the possibility of human consciousness? How does he do what he does? And so on.

"Miracle Stories"

Now that is what is known in the trade as a miracle story. A miracle story is a miracle story. They're lovely, and you can say, "Oh, isn't that remarkable?" Westerners usually have their minds blown by miracle stories, because we read about miracles in the Bible, but usually we say, "Well, that's all fine for them, but now who knows whether the hysteria of those people didn't . . ." you know that place? Though I've written about it in *Be Here Now*, perhaps I'll just review one other thing, which was the way in which I met this man, and that will give you just a little more insight into some of the exquisitry of it all.

The first time I had gone to India, which was in 1967, I had gone because I had been working since 1961 primarily in the realm of human consciousness and what consciousness or awareness was about and what the possibilities were, and the nature of the inner experiences connected with consciousness and what are called altered states of consciousness, and by 1966 or 1967, though I was a writer and lecturer in the field of consciousness-expansion and knew the literature and knew most of the people who were doing research in the West, and had ingested psychedelic chemicals extensively, it appeared to me at the time that whatever it was that we knew, we certainly didn't know enough. We didn't know *really* what it was about. It just—the literature from the East—made it seem possible that somebody at some time had known the stuff we were trying to find out. But the problem was that often you just couldn't understand what it was you were reading about. And various of my friends had gone to India and they'd come back and they'd said, "Well, it's all sort of nice historically, but it doesn't seem to be the living tradition. You can't find the real thing now. Probably all those guys that knew are gone." So I went to India, not because I thought I was going to find anything, but because I didn't know what else to do.

By that time I had been fired from Harvard for LSD research; I had used up lecturing about drugs because I knew I didn't know. What was the sense in lecturing about it if you didn't know? The hypocrisy was too horrible. And we made an extensive tour—I was with a very wealthy man—in a Land

Rover through India. Finally found nothing. I mean, we took wonderful slides, made exquisite tape recordings—beautiful Indian music, nice cross-cultural type study. Got to Katmandu, Nepal—ready to give up. Then I met this young Westerner who was a very extraordinary being, and I realized in some way— although he was very young and was originally from Laguna Beach and so on—that this fellow knew something that I didn't know. And I started to follow him in India. In the course of following him, after about three months I had decided, well, that was enough of that. I had been on a temple pilgrimage and I decided to return to America, and I was going to stay a little longer, and he had to extend his visa, and we were in a small city, and then he said, "I have to go to the mountains to see my guru." I thought that this was a Hindu guru, and my whole leaning was toward Buddhism because Buddhism is very neat and clean and intellectually exquisite, and Hinduism generally is kind of sloppy. You know those posters of Hinduism: the colors are kind of garish and the whole thing turns you off. A little too gauche for my taste . . . too maudlin emotional. So I didn't want to go see a Hindu guru in the Himalayas. That seemed to me like kind of a waste of a trip, and furthermore he wanted to use this Land Rover which had been left in India by this wealthy man. I didn't want the responsibility of it, but he insisted, and so we did this, and I sort of sat in the front seat and I sulked all the way up into the mountains. He wouldn't even let me drive. I mean, it was one of those horrible things.

Now the previous evening I had been staying in this home in Lucknow, and during the night I went out under the stars to go to the bathroom, and I thought about my mother. As I looked up, the stars were very close and clear. My mother had died six months previously in Boston at the Peter Brent Brigham Hospital from a spleen condition in which it enlarged tremendously, and then they removed it and she died from leukemia. I didn't think of her in any positive or negative sense, or anything. I just felt her presence and I just was aware of her at that time. I hadn't thought of her for some months at that time. Then I went back to bed.

The next day we got in the Land Rover. We drove up to the mountains. We got up to this little temple by the side of the road. The car stopped. I thought it was just stopping to let a truck pass, but as it stopped people surrounded the car and this fellow obviously knew what was happening. He had been crying all the way up into the mountains. I felt it was obviously some important emotional thing for him. But I was very paranoid and not interested at all. He asked where this man Maharaj-ji was, and they said up on a hill, and he went running up the hill. I was running behind him, and the absurdity of my position struck me. Here was this young Westerner running up to see this Hindu holy man of the mountains, and I am a—you know, he's just a high school graduate nut, and here I am an ex-Harvard professor, running up this hill barefoot behind this guy, and I must be crazy. You know there is something absolutely insane about that. I get to the top of the hill, and there's this old man sitting with a blanket, and about eight or nine Indian people sitting around. This fellow, this young Westerner, is lying flat out on his face touching this man's feet and he's crying and the man's patting him on the head. I come up and I take a look at this, and I think, Well I'm not going to do that. I mean, I don't know what else you got to do here, but Hindu guru or not—after all, I'm just a visitor, I'm just a tourist in a car, and I don't have to get that involved. I'll just sort of mind my own business. So I am sort of standing in the far, remote part of the field watching the scene. You know, I'm doing a sociological . . . and he looks up at me and he says, in Hindi—I understand sort of pidgin Hindi, and then it's translated also—he says to me, "You came in a big car?" Now, I realize that where we are in the mountains you can't see the road, but I assume somebody rushed up and said, "Here come these people in a big car." But you've got to understand that the car is a source of great upset to me. First of all, because my other friend is so rich and it's not my car, and I don't want the responsibility of this thing; because a $7,000 Land Rover, a special deluxe Land Rover, is probably the fanciest car in all of India—it's equal to half the economy of India, practically. So I'm very uptight about the car, and he just touches that thing. He says, "You came in a big car?" So I said, "Yes." That was his opening gambit. Then he said to me, "You give it to me?" Well, that's a peculiar question. You know—I mean, it's not my car and I come out of a Jewish tradition. My father used to be head of the United Jewish Appeal, and I know how to raise money, but I've never seen a hustle like this. I mean, I don't even know the guy's name and he's already asking me for a $7,000 vehicle. He's not even being nice to me. So I said, "Well . . ." I want to say no, but this young fellow looks up and says, "Maharaj-ji, if you want it, it's yours." I said to him, "But you can't, you know, it's David's car, you can't"— and everybody's laughing at me, the whole group is laughing at me, and I don't know what's funny. So the paranoia is rising at an incredible rate. I'm just getting more and more uptight. Then he said to me, "You made much money in America?" "Yeah"—now he's playing on my ego a little bit, you see, that's a little ego-feeding. "How much did you make?" So I thought of one of my really good years, you know, and I added a little here and there. I don't remember. I think I said $25,000. Well, he converted that into rupees, which of course totally devastated the whole scene. They couldn't even conceive of anybody making that much money. So he looked at me and he says, "You'll buy a car like that for me?" I mean, you may not give me this one, but you got all this money, you'll buy one for me? So I said, "Well, maybe, I don't know." I was trying to play it cool. So then he says, "Jao, jao," go away.

We were taken away, and we were given this food, this boy and I. This boy knows very little about my past. We never talk about it. We sing holy songs together. He was never particularly interested in my past. And I wouldn't discuss my inner thoughts or anything with him—it just never was relevant. After we take food and a little rest, I'm called back to this man and he says, "Come, sit down here." So I sit down. He looks at me and he says, "You were out under the stars last night." So I try to remember and I think, no, I wasn't. Oh yes, I went out to go to the bathroom. "Yes, I was out under the stars." He said, "You were thinking about your mother." Well, now, that's pretty good, see, because I didn't tell anybody that; how could he know that? It could be a lucky guess, but I wasn't thinking about it at the moment. I said, "Yes." He said to me, "She died last year." "Yeah." He closed his eyes. "She got very big in the belly before she died." That was the spleen—this enlarged spleen. I said "Yeah." This is all in Hindi. And he closed his eyes and he suddenly looked me directly in the eye and he said in English, "Spleen." Now the effect of that was very interesting. Because when you hear something in Hindi and it's translated it doesn't have the same impact as when you hear the word in English, especially the thing that was the cause of my mother's death being handed to me with this man looking me directly in the eye. What happened, in effect, was that my mind went fast—first I got totally paranoid. I mean, I assumed suddenly that I was in a science fiction scene, and this was the head of the world interpol or something, and he'd press a button in the earth and the ground would open and a file would come out, and they had brought me here, and, you know, this was a huge plot to take me over. But the plot was too absurd, I mean, my mind couldn't handle that. Finally my mind went until it just sort of—gave up. You know, the red light goes on and it says, "Tilt," or "Reject," or "This program is not compatible with the data you are feeding in," or something like that, because none of my programs handled what he had just done to me.

At that point there was a simultaneous experience which was an incredible one of a very violent, very painful wrenching in my chest which was like a door long closed being opened— one of those squeaking heavy doors being scrunched open— and I started to cry and the crying was neither sad nor happy. The closest I could feel was, "I'm home." Now you could say he was my father and I was coming back to the good father, and he *knew*. I could finally realize that somebody knew. It might have been that reassurance, I don't know. But at any rate the tears came.

I went back that night to a house nearby, and during the evening I was very confused. I didn't know what had happened to me. They were sort of taking care of me. At one point I was into my shoulder bag which I was carrying. I was looking in there, and I found this little bottle of LSD. I had brought that to India—not because I was particularly eager to take it, since I had taken it up to here as far as I was concerned, but because I thought I might meet somebody who I could give it to who would tell me something about what it was all about. I thought, "After all, I'll give it to these holy men," and I'd give it to different holy men like a Buddhist monk and I'd say "How did it affect you, sir?" and he'd say, "It gave me a headache." I'd give it to somebody else and they'd say, "Well, it is good for meditation." Somebody else said, "Well, meditation is better than this." Somebody else said, "Where can I get more?" There was the standard set of reactions that you'd get in the West. You didn't have to go to India to find out all those reactions. So I found this bottle and I thought, "Gee—you know, *this* guy is going to *know*. I'll talk to him about LSD."

I go to bed. The next morning a message comes: Maharaj-ji wants to see you. We go over to the temple around 7:30 or 8 in the morning. I'm walking toward him. I'm about as far from him as that booth back there, and he yells at me, "Where's the medicine?" I'm not used to thinking of LSD as medicine, so I was a little confused. I said, "Medicine? What medicine?" He said, "The medicine, the medicine." I said, "LSD?" "Yes, bring the medicine." So I went to the car and I got the medicine and I brought it back.

"Let me see." So I put it on my hand. I had all different kinds of things in there. "What's that?" I said, "LSD." "What's that?" "That's mescaline, that's librium, and that's"—you know, a little traveling kit. So he said, "Does it give you *siddhis*?" Now *siddhis* in India means "powers." But I had never heard the word before. It means spiritual powers, and since I never heard the word before and they translated it as powers, I thought he wanted like vitamin B-12. You see, I figure he's an old man, he must be losing his power and he wants vitamin B-12 and I didn't have vitamin B-12, so I said, "I'm sorry—no, this doesn't give you that kind of power," and I put it back in the bottle. He says, "Nay, nay," and he holds out his hand. So I put one pill in his hand. These pills were 300 micrograms each. He looked at it. "Come on." So I put a second one—that was 600 micrograms. He looked, so I put a third pill on—that was 900 micrograms—which seemed like an adequate dose for anyone—and he went like that, see, took all three pills—and I was around him all that morning, and nothing at all happened. Like, "That's your medicine, groovy, that's interesting." Nothing happened at all.

Now it's interesting that I came back to America after that and I told many people and in fact published it and said that this man had taken 900 micrograms of LSD and nothing had happened. But all the time I was saying this, there was a gnawing doubt in my mind. Just a tiny little one that maybe, since I was so confused at that time, maybe what he did—he took the pills and he threw them over his shoulder, you know, and it was all a magical thing, and he'd never taken them at all. So it is interesting to follow the sequence through, since now we can see another round this time when I'm back in India. One day he calls me up to him and he says, "Say, did you give me any medicine last time you were in India?" I said, "Yeah." He said, "Did I take it?" I said, "Well, I think so." "Oh. Did it have any effect on me?" I said, "No, I don't think so." He said, "Oh. Go away." So I went away and the next morning I received a call from him and he says, "You got any more of that medicine?" I said, "Yeah." "Bring it." So I bring it. I have what is comparable to 1,500 micrograms. I put it on his hand, and one pill is broken and he gives that back to me. The rest he is holding in his hand, and this time, as if in response to my slight doubt, he takes each one—and he does it *very carefully* to make sure that I see that it is going into his mouth and he is swallowing it, you see. After he swallows all these pills, he looks at me as if panicked and he says, "Pani—can I take water?" And I said, "Sure." He asks, "Hot or cold?" and I said, "Either one, it doesn't matter." He's calling, "Pani, Pani, bring water, bring water." They bring a glass of water and he drinks it down. Then he says, "How long will it take to act? How long will it take?" I said, "Well, I don't know, about an hour or—something will happen in an hour, I'm sure." So he calls a man over and he has a man with a wristwatch and he's holding the man's wristwatch and he says to me, "Will it make me crazy?" And our relationship is very intimate so I said to him, "Probably!" So at this point he goes under his blanket, which is what he sits with, and he comes up looking absolutely insane! At which point I think, "Aha, oh, what have I done? I've let this old man take this strong drug and now he's gone crazy—oh, what a terrible—it'll be an international incident, and it's terrible, and I've blown it again." Then he laughed at me—and at the end of an hour, just nothing had happened. And I was there all day and nothing had happened at all. At the end of the hour he says, "You got anything stronger?" I said no. "Oh." And he said these substances were known about in the Kulu Valley, long ago, but all that knowledge is lost now. Then he said, "It's useful, it's useful, not the true *samadhi*, but it's useful." Then later when questioned about LSD by some of the young Westerners that were with him, he said, "If you're in a cool place and you're quiet and you're feeling much peace and your mind is turned toward God, it's useful. It's useful." He said it will allow you to come in and have the visit—the *darshan*—of a saint, of a higher being of a higher space—higher consciousness is how you can translate it. But he says you can't stay there—after a couple of hours you gotta come back. He said, you know, it would be much better to become the saint, rather than to go and have his visit; but having his visit is nice. He said it strengthens your faith in the possibility that such beings exist. At the time he used Christ as the saint he was talking about. He said it allows you to have the visit of Christ but you can't stay with him. It would be better to become like Christ than to visit, and LSD won't do that for you. He said it will strengthen your faith but it won't make you into that. He said love is a much stronger drug than LSD medicine.

One day I had my Volkswagen microbus, and I went to visit a little temple with about six or eight other people because he had said to come at one in the afternoon. On the way back we crossed a bridge over a river and went up a hill, and the Volkswagen wouldn't get up the hill. So I told everybody to get out and push. Everybody got out but the women—the three women—and I thought, "Gee, they're young and healthy —why don't they get out and push?" But I just thought it—I didn't say it. We pushed and we got to the temple and we walked in and Maharaj-ji looked and he said "Ram Dass is angry." Everyone said, "No, he's not angry, Maharaj-ji." "Yes, he's angry because the women wouldn't get out and push." Now if you can imagine having someone like that who's in your head like that—I mean, where am I going to hide? Many of us have been through psychoanalysis—I've been through five years of it and I can tell you that as exquisite as the game is, there's always subtle ways to hide. But where am I going to hide now from this guy? He obviously can see—he can see my inner head thoroughly at a distance and at any time.

What effect did that have on me? Who is he? What kind of a being is this? What is this phenomenon? How is this working? How does he do it? In the past four or five years when I have really steeped myself in Hindu and Buddhist doctrine and techniques, it has become apparent to me that in many of the some three-hundred-odd LSD trips that I've taken I have touched many, many, many, of the places that are described in the literature. For example, the reason that we translated the *Tibetan Book of the Dead* and published it as *The Psychedelic Experience* back in 1964 was because the nature of the experiences in the *Bardo Thodol*—the stages, the bardo—the stages one goes through in the process of death—that a Tibetan has read to him by a Tibetan lama at the time he is dying—those descriptions of the different planes or states of consciousness—many of those descriptions were the most vivid descriptions of what we were experiencing with psychedelics, but hadn't been able to describe. We were saying it was ineffable, and there it was, described in this book that was 2,500 years old. So whatever they were talking about was certainly similar to whatever it was that we were playing with—LSD.

It's true that in terms of the nature of the experiences that I've had from study and meditation and being in India for these past few years, there are very, very dramatic parallels. Those of you who have had psychedelics know that the stuff goes through so fast. There's so much of it that all that stays in is these little bits of total conscious momentary fragments of planes and experiences—sitting there but not necessarily conceptually able to be organized—and when you start to read these Hindu descriptions of the way of the gods, the Devas, the planes of consciousness—the different loci they're called— you suddenly realize, "Oh, yeah, that was that experience I had in Zihuatanejo," or, "That was that experience I had in . . ." you know, wherever, at that moment. Suddenly the pieces start falling into place and you realize that the Easterners have had exquisite conceptual maps of consciousness for a lot of the stuff that we are incredibly interested in at the moment. Fascinated with, I might say. There's a very funny side. Buddha said, "The smallest unit of energy is called the *kalapas*," and he said, "There are one trillion *kalapas* per blink of an eye that are born and die in sequence." O.K., one trillion. Now that would seem like a very melodramatic statement— certainly one gauged for public relations, words like "one trillion" and "blink of an eye" and so on. But it is interesting that about four or five years ago the Nobel prize in physics was won by a man who with a linear accelerator and cyclotron measured the light span of the tiniest unit that they can get a trace on, and the time—although it's not in blinks of eyes, as you might imagine, but more like in seconds of milliseconds—comes out to be almost identical with that which Buddha stated 2,500 years ago, roughly a trillion per blink of an eye. Then Buddha said, "That's all very interesting, but the human mind has seventeen mind moments for every *kalapas*." That means there are seventeen trillion thoughts per blink of an eye, in sequence.

NIRVANA

Now I'll take you the next step out as long as we are in the science fiction world. It's all contained in a huge book of the Southern Buddhist literature called the *Tripitaka* and the *Visuddhimagga* which is part of the *Tripitaka* and is a description of a certain kind of meditation. In the *Visuddhimagga* he describes the thirty-four last mind moments before you go into nirvana. I mean, out of seventeen trillion, he's describing thirty-four of them—one by one—and then the nirvanic state is placed between two mind moments—between two of the seventeen trillion. That's the game we're dealing with. Now just assume Buddha is just like us—what is the potential of human awareness in relation to the rate of thought and the ability to focus on specific mind moments or single thought units? It's interesting, because many of us who have taken various psychedelic chemicals have experienced a speeding up of thought. Actually, all it is is an awareness that gets more discriminative, and you are just seeing more of your thought moments. But even then, you are seeing it at an incredibly gross level compared to this kind of discipline of being able to move awareness behind thought and observe sequences of your own thoughts, and be able to be calm enough and detached enough from your own thought to witness thoughts.

Buddha describes these stages of the arising of a thought, the duration of it and the dying of it. Now there are seventeen trillion per mind moment and he describes at one moment that you just focus on the arising of thoughts and you look around and it looks as if the whole universe is being created over again. That's Christ's statement, "Look, I am making all things new." It's that thing where it's all just appearing—many of you I am sure have had that experience—and then there's another one where he says you suddenly are aware only of the dissolution of each moment. It's as if everything is dying or decaying, because Buddha says, in effect, every mind moment is an entire universe and between moments there is nothing, as far as you're concerned. So, in effect, when you experience anything as simultaneous, it really isn't simultaneous at all. It's just that the rate of it makes you experience synchronicity simultaneously—but it isn't really. Like you think you're hearing me and at the same moment seeing me. But you're not—it's like going through your five senses and your thinking mind —it's just "brrrrr"—like that. It's just collating, and collating, and collating, and giving you these kinds of summary print-outs. Now if any being was ever capable of purifying and quieting awareness sufficiently and directing it in a laser beam technique sufficiently to be able to examine his own thoughts, one by one, which go at this incredible rate—what is the capacity of human awareness?

"EASTERN" AND "WESTERN" MODELS OF MAN

What I'm going to continue to say is even much further out than this, so I want you to be grounded in like, you know, the scientific questions, before it gets too far out, because I'm going to share with you who I think this guy really is that I am visiting in India. I've been around him for five years and I've done little else but think about him. It's like having one case study and just studying him and studying him and thinking about him and sitting at his feet and looking at him and listening to everything he says, and after all, no matter how many drugs I've taken there's still some level, I'm sure you can hear, where I'm a social scientist. I mean, I was trained. I know chi squares and analysis of variance and factor analytic techniques and all that stuff—I'm still right here. And that kind of training has made me, at the same moment as I'm a drunken *bhakti*—an emotional devotee, it's called—at the same moment, there's a little computer mind in me, you know. It's like—when he took the LSD the first time, the thought that ran through my mind at that moment was, "This is going to be interesting." Now that's a scientific speculation thought, right? That guy is still in me, too.

One of the basic differences between Eastern and Western models of man—and this is not an "Eastern" and "Western" cop-out, really—it isn't that. There are many different ways of saying that. You could say, one that comes out of philosophical materialism versus one that comes out of the mystic tradition. I mean, there are many ways of saying it. But the basic difference can be exemplified by the statement *Cogito, ergo sum*, "I think, therefore I am." Now at one level that's true, because a thought is the way in which you "know the universe." But the basic distinction is that who you are is not an identity with your thoughts. That is, *I think, but I am not my thoughts*. And that becomes a very critical place. A critical place. For example, in meditation there are meditative exercises which involve extricating yourself from attachment to your senses. Now, you know for example—for many of you this is old hat, but I'll go through this systematically. Many of you for example have had the experience where you are reading a book, and you are so involved in reading the book that you don't hear somebody come in the room. Nevertheless you know as a sophisticated individual that the air—we didn't put ear plugs in—the air is operating, the auditory nerves are functioning, the sound waves are coming, the transmission is occurring, it's going somewhere. But you could say that whoever you are wasn't attending to that at the moment. So the air was functioning, but you weren't attending to your air. Well, in the same way there are ways of not attending to your eyes seeing, your nose smelling, your tongue tasting and your skin feeling.

Now imagine that instead of just this random thing completely out of control, where at times you happen not to hear something that goes by, imagine that there were a way, through discipline—which is what meditation is about—of extricating yourself from these senses so that they go on doing their processes. They go on working, but you are no longer busy processing those data. They're just going through but you're not involved. What's left? After all, at that point it's like an anesthetic—you're not experiencing your body, you're not hearing things coming from the outside world, you're not seeing things, although your eyes are open. You're not tasting anything, or smelling it. Well, what's left are your thoughts—what you're thinking. In the meditative exercises the sequence goes—"I am not my body, I am not my organs, I am not my senses," and the final one, the one right at the end of the whole journey is, "I am not this thought." Which thought aren't you? I am not the thought. I am not the thought. I am not the thought. You got that place? I mean, it takes you way out on a limb.

This is called *Atma-Vichara*, and it comes out of the exquisite consciousness of Ramana Maharshi. Finally you get way, way out on a tiny limb, when all you're left with is your own thoughts, and then you say, "No, not that either." In the Indian philosophy it's called *neti, neti*—no, not that—no, not that—no, not that—no, not that either—no, not that—and you're constantly separating. Is this too heavy? How we doing? I should get feedback, because I don't want to overload the circuits. It would be irrelevant.

The meditation that I do, for example, is called *vipassana* meditation. It's from the Southern Buddhists and it's a very simple exercise. It's the exercise of bringing your mind to one point. They use the analogy in India that it's like trying to take an elephant that has been wild in the jungle and putting one of those iron bands around its leg and then sticking a post in the ground to tame it. When the elephant suddenly realizes that you are trying to tame it, it gets wilder than it ever was at its wildest in the jungle, and it pulls at its leg and it can hurt its leg. It could break its leg, it starts to bleed, it does all kinds of things before it finally gives in and becomes tame. And this roughly is the tradition of meditation.

Vivekananda, one of the Eastern people who came to the West and taught this, said, "The mind is a terrible master and it's a wonderful servant." But for most of us it is our master and not our servant. We are so identified with our own thoughts. So this process is the process of bringing your mind to one point. Now, let me tell you to—well, for just like, say, fifteen seconds—play this little game. Just do what I do. Let me explain. I go into ten-day courses where sixteen hours a day, this is what I do. We'll do it for fifteen seconds. You focus right on the tip of your nose and you note the breath going in and out. You don't follow it into your body and you don't follow it out into the *akasa*, into the universe. You just notice it right here. You're like a parking lot attendant. And your job is merely to notice a car that goes in the factory and one that goes out. You don't care where it went or who, you know, you're just a checker. Just check—it went in and that one came out. This one goes in—ah—there's one coming out. That's all you do—you just sit right there and notice it. That's all you do— you just sit right there and notice it. That's all you've got to do. We'll just do it for fifteen seconds. During that time don't think about anything else.

You can at least get a feeling for what the game is. Now imagine that you are a sophisticated, rational, Western person and you go into a course and you sit down and the man says, "All right, I honor you and you honor me and we all honor each other, and we're sitting. Everybody comfortable? Fine! All right, now, for the next sixteen hours with breaks every forty minutes to walk around the room a couple of times, you will just follow this breath going in and out of your nose." Well, you literally psychologically climb the walls. I'll tell you. I mean, if you thought you had any discipline of mind, you see what you don't have, very, very, very quickly. See, like most of you probably heard the air conditioner, or you felt your body or you thought, "What the hell's this all about?" or, "Isn't this in- teresting?" or, "My," or you know, "I can't even find my breath." Everybody's got these little "brrrr" thoughts. They're like little mosquitoes buzzing around.

What happens is you usually sit down and meditate and you start in, and then—what I go through, what I used to go through (I don't any more), I'd start in and I'd think—"Ah, this feels good." That's a thought. That's not part of the game, see. What you do with every thought, when it comes up—it's like somebody who drops by for tea when you are trying to work on a manuscript. You say, "Hello, it's great to have you. Why don't you go into the kitchen and have tea with my wife, and I'll be along later. I'm working on this manuscript." And then you go back to the manuscript.

You sit down and you think, "Right, fine." The next thing is "Gee, my knee hurts." Thought. Just another thought. For the first few days they are very kind to you. They let you, when your knee hurts, move your knee. Later the instructions are for the next forty minutes you're not to move at all. Your knee hurts, and that's just a stimulus. After all, your knee isn't going to fall apart if it hurts for a while. Each time you deal with pain, you bring your consciousness back. It gets caught again, and you bring it back. If it gets caught, you don't get violent with yourself. You don't beat the elephant. You just constantly remind it that it's hooked to this post in the ground, so you just keep coming back. It's called a primary object. You just keep coming back to the primary object. You go through "My knee hurts." "Oh, I'm hungry"—that's another one. Then there's another one: "For this I got a Ph.D.?" That's a great one, you know, like "What am I doing here? After all this training here I am sitting watching my breath. I mean, I ought to be in a mental hospital." And, "Who sits around all day long watching the breath of their nose?" I mean, its obviously some totally compulsive individual who's afraid he's going to stop breathing or something. And to take that on as a chosen discipline—sixteen hours a day—day after day?

But the funny thing is, we will spend millions and millions of dollars on creating these incredibly complex computers, and filling our mind with knowledge, but the actual tool, which is the tool of our conscious awareness, we spend very little time training. We don't even understand in the West what it *means* to train consciousness, or what it means to develop these disciplines of one point. Because it is literally true that, were you able to keep your consciousness in the same place, on one point—literally on one point for twelve seconds—you would be in one of the highest forms of *samadhi*. You would be one of the most enlightened beings. Twelve seconds, that isn't much. That's how out of control we are. And what it does is, over the course of some days or some weeks you begin to notice your mind operating. You begin to notice how your desires keep manifesting in thoughts. You'll be sitting there and suddenly get incredible sexual rushes and fantasies. Keep in mind now that who you know yourself to be is only a function of your thoughts or your conceptual models of who you are.

Ego is really a conceptual structure of some sort, and if your mind is thinking about the same thing all the time, what happened to the ego? Because the ego is really based on part of those seventeen trillion mind moments being filled with redefining the game—over and over again. "Well, really I'm Ram Dass, really I'm Ram Dass and I'm doing this and I'm somebody who gets hungry and I'm . . . and there's the world out there and I'm here . . . I'm just . . ." We're using all of our senses and our associative stuff to keep the game together—to keep our conceptual framework of the universe in order. The minute you bring your mind in to one point, what in effect you're doing is over-riding the existing program in the computer. And when you do that, there is an incredible amount, of course, of the computer trying to re-assert itself, so that the thoughts get more insistent, more demanding—suddenly you've got to go to the bathroom in the worst way, even though you just went ten minutes ago. There is a book called the *Bhagavad Gita* in India which is a book that is concerned with a battle—supposedly a battle out in the battlefield. But one way of understanding that book is it's this inner battle about who's going to run the game. Are your thoughts going to be your master or are you going to be master of your thoughts? I would like to have programs available, one of which is the Ram Dass Program, but I would like not to have it run my life. Because it turns out that isn't who I am. That's who I thought I was.

Vivekananda talks about a coach going down the road with a coachman and the man inside the coach. For years, the man inside has just been sitting in there, or the woman inside has been sitting there, and the coachman has been running the coach. The coachman has gotten the feeling that the coachman owns the coach and is making all the decisions. Finally the person inside taps on the glass and says, "Say, would you pull over here?" Imagine what happens in the coachman's mind. He never even knew there was anybody back there in the first place, and he is under the impression it's his coach and his horses and he's running the show. And then suddenly this person says, "Would you pull over, here's . . ." "Who the hell do you think you are? It's my coach!" "What do you mean it's your coach?" "Ever since I can remember, ever since I can remember," says the coachman, "I've been running this coach." "Well, I understand that, but now—you know you were going in the right direction—now it's time for a change, and would you mind pulling over?" What do you imagine happens then? I mean the coachman doesn't just say, "Oh, Master, I'm sorry, I give up," and pull over. Then starts the struggle which is outlined in the *Bhagavad Gita*. The struggle of these different forces inside which could be characterized—although it's treading on very thin ice because of the way in which we use words like this—but it could be talked about as the ego, or the conceptual framework of separate identity versus consciousness. I'll talk a little more about what that consciousness is about, although I know that some of you use the term ego in different ways.

What happens is that when you try to bring your mind to one point, at first it speeds up incredibly and each thought is saying, in effect, "Think of me, think of me, I'm important,

I'm important." Like, "What was that noise outside?" You know, "I've got to get up—oh, I forgot to call so and so." I mean you can't imagine what comes up. If you really want to take somebody to another level of consciousness just put them in a room; this is what I do when I run a training center. I have these domes out in New Mexico that are just domes out in the woods, and they are totally empty. They have a little wood fire and a bottle of water and I take a person, give him a sleeping bag and put him in there and close the door. Food is left outside every day and they can go to the bathroom, go back in. It's a totally empty room and they are left there for anywhere up to nineteen days.

That's a very interesting experience because there is nowhere you can hide. You can't hide in books. You can't hide in collecting more experiences. What you start to do is run your old tapes. You remember—I used to sit and think about all the people I ever knew and I'd go back to kindergarten, and all the people I had ever known. Then I'd take one of them and try to remember all the things about him. Then I'd go through all the best restaurants that I've ever eaten in in my life. Then I'd go through all the places I still wanted to visit, then I'd go through all my theoretical models of what I thought was happening, and I *still* had days left. The mind would just keep creating this stuff and this stuff and this stuff. I was doing this in a temple in India and—after all, I had closed the door of the temple, this was a voluntary thing.

And every day at four o'clock the bus would go by, and I could just see out my window this bus that went to Delhi going by. And from there I could get an airplane to America. Sometimes at 3:30 in the afternoon when I knew the bus was going to go by at four I'd think, "What the hell am I doing here?" I could just grab my clothes and leave a note and within two days I would be dancing at the Fillmore—I mean I could be like back in life. "What am I doing, what kind of idiocy is this?" You know, I mean I would create this stuff and I would be just pacing around the room like a mad, wild man.

The last time I was in India I went into seclusion in a place where they lock you in and put food in through a double window. They open the window and put the food in and close it. You don't ever see a human being at all and it's complete—there's no windows, nothing. And I was naked in there all the time. It was very hot, down in the southern part of India. And when I got out I went to my guru and the first thing he said to me is, "It's good not to wear clothes when you're in there meditating." So you think you're alone. . . . So you try to bring your mind down and quiet your mind and of course these thoughts get more and more dramatic and more and more crisisey and more and more pulling and the most vicious thoughts are the thoughts, "This is never going to work." That's a good one and the other kind of thought that hangs you up is, "It's working." See what happens is you're doing it and you quiet your mind just a little and you get these incredible rushes. You get these ecstatic feelings of incredible bliss—even to incredible calm. And you've never felt this kind of "ahhh." Of course, all those experiences are just more thoughts.

All those experiences are just more thoughts. "Oh, got me again. Got me again." They are more subtle all the time. They keep taking you just where you least expect them to. And it's only after some time that you stop drinking in the ecstasy or stop going through the struggles and you start to get calmer and calmer and calmer and let the mind *just sit quietly* and do its thing. It's the awareness which starts to approach what the Buddhists call "pure mind." The thoughts are still there but they are floating by just like clouds. They're not grabbing at you. Now, the question of why thoughts arise is concerned with human motivation. Motivation is what in the Eastern tradition is called attachment or desire—clinging—and attachment or desire or clinging is the root of the problem. Now here's my predicament, see. I was trained as a motivation psychologist, right? Dave McClelland was my boss, and I worked in the field of achievement motivation, dependency motivation, nurturance, succorance, power, affiliation, etc., sexual hunger, thirst, the drives and needs. I used to teach courses in human motivation.

I come from a tradition where, from a psychological point of view, motives are "givens" in man. Everybody's got drives and needs and so on. Now I come into a tradition where motives are seen not as necessary things, but as part of the package, if you will—*not who you are*. As a motivation psychologist, I defined who we are in terms of motivation. Now I'm seeing that motivation is part of the package, but it isn't who we are. This is a very critical place, very critical.

When Buddha came out from under the Bodhi tree where he got enlightened, he came back to the guys he'd been hanging out with and he said "Hey, fellas, I figured it all out." And he gave them what is called the Four Noble Truths. The first truth is, "It's all suffering." That's a hard one for us in the West. What do you mean, it's all suffering? It's not all suffering. I had a wonderful time last night. But the breakdown of the statement "It's all suffering" is as follows: birth has in it suffering, death has in it suffering, old age has in it suffering, and sickness has in it suffering. Not getting what you want has in it suffering; getting what you don't want has in it suffering. We'll all agree to all those, which leaves two categories—getting what you want and not getting what you don't want—which we don't include under the category of suffering.

Then he says, "But you see, about those two—they are both in time, and *anything* in time is going to go." I've used the example of the ice cream cone. You know, you start to eat the ice cream cone and you got to keep eating cause it's going to melt and you can't keep that first rush of the ice cream cone forever because after a while you are going to have had enough ice cream cone and you already know it when you take your first bite so even in the first bite of the ice cream cone is the suffering of the anticipation that it's going to be over. That's true about sex, and it's true about everything you ever wanted. Like, "We'd like to advise you, you've just been given the Nobel Prize for the greatest contribution to science this year!"

"Oh, thank you." "Would you make a statement?" And the first question the reporters ask you is, "What is your next project?" You don't even have a moment to stop and say, "Oh boy, I've just won the Nobel." Or, the whole thing about the achievement ladder we're all very familiar with.

I used to hang out with the Mellon Family. The Mellon family is very rich. Each of the parents has 700 million dollars. That's rich in my book. The kids were poor. They each had only 20 million. I hung out with one of these kids who had 20 million dollars and he felt like a bum. I had a little Cessna plane and we'd land it in New York and we'd pull up next to this very fancy jet at the private-run place. He'd say, "That's Uncle Paul's. Gee, I really wish I could afford that." Here's a guy with 20 million dollars who's miserable. Right! That's far out, from my point of view. You know, I remember spending a weekend with Hugh Heffner in his Playboy house in Chicago. And there was suffering in the midst of plenty, I assure you. In the midst of plenty—suffering. That's what Buddha was talking about. As long as you are in time—there's suffering.

Then his second noble truth is: the cause of suffering is craving. The reason you suffer is because you want something.

His third noble truth is: if you didn't want anything, you wouldn't suffer. If you give up wanting something, you won't suffer.

And the fourth noble truth is what is called the Eight-fold Path—to give up wanting anything you have to give up wanting it. What relevance could an Eight-fold Path have if you're a human motivation expert who assumes that who you are are your motives? What's going to be left if you give them up? Or, who you are is your personality. That's why it's all so interesting. Because it turns out that as you get deeper into this study of what your awareness is—through your own experience and through meditation—you begin to see that who you are doesn't turn out to be your personality. It doesn't even turn out to be any of your motivational or perceptual structures. It's like, I see, but I am not "seeing." I know, but I am not the same as knowing—but I know. I think. I think. The predicament is that when I say "I think," the term "I," to conceptualize "I," *is* a thought.

We can imagine what it's like to be extricated from social motives, like the need for external loves or achievement or affiliation and so on. But what about food and water and stuff like that? Here I go—this is where it gets very science fiction again because in India the people I live with often—their actual living experiences—make a total shambles of our Western models of health. I studied with a man whose total input of food for fifteen years—and this is not my guru, but a teacher of mine—his total input was two glasses of milk a day. He had more energy than I had, and certainly more than most of the people I had ever met. He slept roughly two hours a night and we'd go up to a mountain—he'd be running up and I'd be trying to kind of pull myself along. He weighed ninety pounds. Totally exquisite in his movements. Two glasses of milk a day. You know what the World Health Organization would say about that? I mean, even if it's good, rich buffalo milk. You're not going to live through it. But there he is. There he is.

All you've got to do is find one guy, see—just one woman or one man who's doing it—and it makes a shambles of the whole trip. The relation of mind to matter is so much more exquisite, and the only way man is able to play with these games is when he has extricated his awareness from his thinking and sensing. Then his awareness becomes just like a laser beam, and it develops a kind of power that is capable of things we don't attribute as possible to human beings. For that power to be developed, however, Buddha points out that you must extract yourself from attachment. That's a very tricky concept—what it means to be free of attachment. In the same way you watch your senses, you watch your eyes see and you watch the desires being manifested, but you no longer identify with your own desires. Just to carry that previous thing I was telling you about—the health business—one step further: there are many very, very clear, documented instances in India of a being who is buried alive for a period of time and after a year or two is brought back and they come out of the state of trance they have been in, and there they are—and they were put in an airproof box. One of them, when asked, "Well, how did you breathe?" said, "My cells had enough oxygen to keep my brain and my heart muscle alive, and that was all that was necessary." And this one that said this—they had put him in the earth in a box, and there were some ants, and the ants had eaten away part of his arm. He had been in this trance, see. . . . So where are human drives, let alone our social motives? I mean, don't you need air, and food? I mean, after all, we assume those are all necessary.

Raising the Kundalini

I used to do a thing called *pranayam*, which is a technique for raising energy up your spine. It's called raising the *Kundalini*. It's a very delicate technique. I used to fast nine days on the new moon. This was when I was doing very intense *sadhana* about five years ago. I would do hatha yoga for a long time, then I would do *pranayam* which is a series of exercises. Some of them are like oxygenation, going on for some minutes. Then there's another one in which you take the air in one nostril tighten up certain muscles halfway between your genitals and your anus, and pull up on certain nerves. It's like you're closing the sphincter of your anus. You pull up on those, and then you take in a breath on a certain count in one nostril and then you close your chin, which closes another place up here. So you close both places, and you bring this together, and you hold your breath, and you hold your breath for longer and longer periods of time over some months, and you get up to a minute and a half or two minutes, and then you learn how to force your attention on the tip of your spine and to visualize right in from the tip of the spine, which is called in the Indian energy system the first *chakra*. You learn to focus on a triangle of

128

flame in which there is a serpent wound with its head down three and a half times around a lingam or a phallus.

You put your whole attention down there. You know when you dive under water or something like that, you hold your breath and then you can't hold your breath any longer, and at that moment you are totally preoccupied with wanting to get air. Now imagine getting to that place then instead of attending to your lungs and that whole melodrama that's going on up here, you put all your attention at the bottom of your spine, and you have sufficient discipline to put it there and keep it there, and what incredible thing happens is that when you can take your attention away from the holding of the breath, you go into this state where you are not breathing, and you are not holding your breath. Usually the awareness of that brings you back. You say, "My God, I'm not breathing!" And that brings you down. But after a while, when you stop getting hysterical about what's happening, you can go into this state and just sit. You're not doing any breathing. You're just sitting with your mind totally focused on your spine, and you've flipped into this place where you're perfectly calm but there is no breath, and at that point you feel this energy pouring up your spine and up into your head. It's very incredible, powerful, and very delicate and must be done very, very delicately, with much guidance—but it's an extraordinary process. But again, from your own personal experience, it knocks to hell your models about who needs to breathe how much.

Maharaj-ji

Now let me share with you who I think that guru is and what I think he's about. Now just follow the sequence. If you were to take your consciousness and bring it out of your senses and out of your thinking mind and bring it down into awareness, what then? Who would you then be? Well, what you would be at that point is awareness. Just awareness, or consciousness. But you're not aware of anything. You're just awareness. Now what is Awareness or Consciousness? This is where the whole dance gets so incredibly far out that it boggles our mind. Usually we can't handle it. It's like Einstein saying, "I didn't arrive at my understanding of the fundamental laws of the universe through my rational mind." He used the word "intuition." Intuition is something we really don't understand, but we use it. We use it when we don't know what else to say about something. We say, "Well, he intuitively knew." Intuitively. Well, what in fact it is, is that there are other ways of man knowing things than through his senses and through his thinking mind. But we don't know how to use them. That is the difference. Our thinking mind and our senses know things as objects. *I know that.* But there are a whole range of things that we know in the sense that we work with them all the time, but we don't *know* them in that way. For example, if you close your eyes and try to describe or try to think about how you make a fist, you'll find out that how you make a fist is really not a conceptual thought, but you make this fist. You are able to make a fist, but you don't necessarily know how you make a fist. And you certainly were able to make a fist long before you could tell how you made a fist—if even now, in your sophistication, you can tell. What I guess I'm saying is that there are ways of subjectively being in the universe so that things are available to you—or in you—that would otherwise only be knowable to you by collecting them through your senses and through your thinking mind.

Now I'll take you to the farthest out places right away, and then we'll play with it just a little. You take this stage I'm on. Look at it—it feels solid. We think of that wood as solid, but we are sufficiently sophisticated—we know that if we subject this to, say, electron microscopy, we will see that it really isn't as solid as it looks. It's actually a whole lot of stuff with big spaces in between. Not only that, but the things that it's made of are actually moving all the time, and when we get down to the tiniest unit of energy, we find out that that unit of energy is just in free flow through it all. Sometimes it's part of that wood, and sometimes it's part of me, and sometimes it's part of this, and there's a total interchange of energy in the universe. All these quanta of energy then go to make up nuclei and electrons and so on. They are all big, gross things compared to this tiny unit of energy which is totally interchangeable in the universe, and seems to flow in what would appear to be a random fashion.

Now, if you can understand that, then what you see as a solid is not really solid. It just looks solid because of the frequency of wavelengths that your eyes are capable of perceiving. You begin to realize—just like with hearing, there is a certain frequency, a range of frequencies that you can hear that are audible, and a dog can hear one you can't hear, and so on. If you were a different receiver mechanism, it would all be quite different to you, because were you tuned up to a different kind of frequency or perceptual sensitivity, everything would look like it was in movement all the time. If you get out further and further in that dimension, you would get to the point where you would see—first of all you would see this stage like a cloud, and you'd see these different entities as clouds, just like you see clouds. They are made of stuff that keeps changing and you would see the cloud, the cloud pattern. Like looking at figures in Rorschach cards. . . . If you go out yet one more level into sensitivity, you would see that these clouds are all part of a solid—you go in more and more until finally when you look at the level of these quanta of energy, the universe is a solid. It's a solid, and everything is interchangeable with everything else. I'm just giving you straight physics—you know, traditional physics now. This isn't any great Eastern mystical discovery—just straight physics.

The Planes of Consciousness

We use higher and higher power microscopes to play these games. And some of us who have had psychedelic experiences have retuned our perceptual apparatus, like a television receiver. Like you and I know that were we to bring in a television receiver and plug it into that plug which just brings electricity in and tune it in, suddenly there'd be someone on channel 3, 4, 5, 9, 10. It all must be here somewhere—but we can't see it. Now, were we able to tune just slightly differently, we could pick it all up. "I think I'll look at channel 3. Now I'll tune to channel 4." Now, that all sounds facetious, but it turns out it isn't at all. That's what are called the planes of consciousness—when you learn how to break attachments enough to channel 7 to be able to tune to channel 6. That's what a guru is talking about—our attachments to a certain channel, or a certain wavelength, or a certain frequency. Now, let us say this being who I am studying with has now extricated himself from all attachment. That means the body is going along in the same way that your heart is beating. He's not sitting around thinking, beat—or peristaltic contraction, right—whup, whup, whup—he's not thinking any of that—it's just going on. It's the same way you drive a car most of the time. It's all in base brain. Most of the time when you're driving you turn on the radio, or look at somebody, or plan your day's events. You couldn't care less. You're making these exquisitely complex adjustments all the time. I mean, hurtling through space—this huge monster, you know, at seventy miles per hour—and you're not even aware you're driving. That's all base brain. Well, imagine now that everything is on base brain. Your eating is on base brain—your sleeping, your talking to people, is all on base brain. All your thinking is on base brain. Ahhh . . . you don't like that one. It's all put on base brain. When the thinking thing needs to happen, it happens. You don't have to worry about it. It's just an associative run-off. Why do you have to spend your time like—you don't have to be that kind of a computer programmer. You could be up doing something else.

If you have extricated yourself completely from all the attachments to this particular frequency—what in the sequence of training happens is, you start to tune to other frequencies. I mean, I have sat with people in India, and I'm sitting next to somebody who is looking at me with their eyes open and my eyes open, and he's talking to somebody I don't see. Now in the

West we put that person in a mental hospital. We say he is hallucinating. But after a while you begin to understand that maybe we don't really quite totally know where it's at, and we put somebody away because they don't play the game the way we play. They don't see it the way we see it. And it turns out that we're hallucinating, too, because we're just fixed on a certain frequency. I have a brother who is often hospitalized and sometimes they let me visit him, but the psychiatrist has to be present. And there's my brother on one plane and the psychiatrist on another plane. They both look crazy, in the sense that they are both attached to what they consider absolute reality. Well, from my point of view these are all relative realities. They are not absolute realities at all. All you have to do is shift in one reality once—you just get out of it once, and suddenly your attachment to what you thought was the real thing starts to collapse pretty fast. You say, "Yes, it's relatively real, but not absolutely real." So that is the training. You go from this plane, and as you loosen your attachments you start to move into other planes which, when we are attached to this plane, we often call hallucinatory states. And sometimes it's very delicate: what's a projection of what.

You come into other frequencies where it all looks different —different greens, different entities—you're looking different. What they call your physical body, your astral body, your causal body, these different bodies are at different frequencies and you're attached to your physical body because you are attached to your senses. When you are attached that way, you don't notice your physical body. So the lowest level of the game is where you loosen the physical body from the astral body.

Let me give you an example of this. I was traveling with a very beautiful swami, Muktananda, on a religious pilgrimage in Southern India. One day about three in the morning he took me by the hand—he's a very powerful swami, very powerful man, very evolved. He took me by the hand, and he took me to a little temple up in the top of the town and he whispered a *mantra* into my ear. That is, it's like a prescription—it's a phrase to be repeated. It's a Sanskrit phrase and Sanskrit is a conscious language—that is, the vibrational sound of each word is meant to do certain things to your nervous system. He recited this thing into my ear and then he did a ceremony over me and I lost my body consciousness, and then a few hours later I was brought back and I came back to him and I said, "What was all that about, Babaji?" He said, "That mantra will give you vast power and vast wealth." And I said to him, "Well, that's great, but I don't want vast power and vast wealth. Unless you promise me an equal amount of love and compassion, forget it." And he says, "Just do the mantra." He's a Shavite, which is very fierce, by the way.

Well, I couldn't not do the mantra. First of all because I wanted power and wealth—no matter what I said I didn't want—and second, because he had put it in so deep I couldn't get rid of the thing. And I was doing it all day and all night, and I was just doing this mantra and doing it and doing it and doing it and doing it. Finally, I came back to his ashram near Bombay and he had me meditate in an inner room, a very special room—they've got to unlock it to let you in. I'm meditating there around 2:30–3 in the morning and I'm lying flat out on the floor, my head back—it's very hot in there— and I'm doing this mantra, and I get taken out of this body and this plane and I'm brought to another plane where there is a room. It would seem that the walls are made of light rather than solid substance, and I come into this room and sitting ahead of me is Swami Muktananda, looking the same as he looks in the physical plane, right? What you call a dream.

I walk in and he looks directly at me and I start to levitate— that is, I start to fly—which is known as a power which is what he promised me, right? The power to fly in my astral body. To leave my body and move, which is a great power in India. So I started to go up in the air and then I started to tilt a little bit and I get a little frightened, see, and I think I'd better right myself, and at that moment I think, "What am

I doing lying on my back?" and I'm back in the room. I was brought back to the physical plane. I get up and I walk out of the meditation room and Muktananda walks up to me and he says, "Enjoy flying?"

Now that is like a tiny example of what astral things are like. I've had many experiences where I've left my body. You can get your body into this, which is called *padmasan*, or the lotus position, and it's perfectly balanced. You can just put your body there and leave and go somewhere—wherever you want to go. You pull yourself back from your senses and from your thinking mind and then, in just the subtle form of your thinking mind, in your astral body, which is this bodiless awareness, you go out. I'll tell you how weird it is, although to talk about this stuff gets very weird for this particular setting. You can look back and you can see the cord of light that links the bodies. It looks like an umbilical cord and it looks like a blue light. Within *that* body is another body, and it gets more and more subtle as you tune your frequency to different planes.

Now imagine that you are not attached to any of these bodies—then what happens to you? Well, that's really what this man is that I meet in India. Because if you are no longer attached at any of the planes. . . . You see, what we call this . . . (taps on floor) . . . when we go down to the quanta of energy, we call it energy. We say these tiny units that are interchangeable in the universe are energy. But now instead of calling them energy, let's call them consciousness, and just say the Universe is Consciousness. Not *self*-consciousness, but consciousness. That is, energy and consciousness are merely two different labels depending on where you are looking at it from. So in effect when he ceases to be the guy sitting in the blanket, and he ceases to be his subtler and subtler forms, what awareness is left, is merely awareness. There is not a separate entity. In the Indian system it is called the *Atman*. There is a *jivatman*, which in Christianity is called the soul, which is the separate entity of higher consciousness. But even that shell breaks and you would say, in effect, the way my guru knows about my mother's spleen, for example—this is really so incredibly far out that it's really hard to say it in front of a group of thinking beings—he knows about my mother's spleen because he is my mother's spleen. He doesn't know he knows about my mother's spleen, and he didn't know he knew about it a minute before he said it, but out of all the possibilities in the universe the thing came through him that was necessary for me at that moment in my life—not by his thinking, "What I think I should do is lay the thing about his mother's spleen on him—that will really blow his mind." You've got to understand there isn't anybody in there. That's the one we can't handle. Now and then when we see a catatonic and we work with him enough we say, "Jesus, maybe there's nobody in there. It's just his body vegetating." Unfortunately, that is a locked-in place on another plane. That isn't the final bag, either. But the predicament is that the consciousness becomes The Consciousness, which is All of It—although at that point you don't know you know anything. Because you *are* it, you don't *know* it. It's the nature of being versus knowing.

This is a very, very delicate thing because our whole educational tradition is that you acquire knowledge through collecting stuff and knowing it. But there was no way he collected that stuff and knew it. About that spleen—a moment later he doesn't even know it. That's what's far out, too. In five years of being with my guru, and thinking about practically nothing but "Who is it?" and "What is this?" I can't yet find anybody home. There's nobody there! There's a personality, but it's not who that person is. I can feel it. You can sense it. You can feel it as you work with it. You think he's the most exquisite mind in the world, and for the next week he is the most stupid old man—bungling, repetitive, dull. You think, "Ufff. Groan. Oh, have I been taken! I'm glad I see the light." Just as you are about to say, "To hell with him, I'm leaving," he does something incredibly mind blowing. You know, when somebody's got a subtle humor that sneaks up on you—you thought you saw the joke and then suddenly—Oh! You see that you didn't see the joke at all. It was another joke. But with him you get to that place and then you know that there are about ten more layers out there, and at every one he's right there saying, "Ah, see the joke." And I get a feeling most of the time like I'm a puppet or a marionette on a string. Do I think that I chose to have the bus go to the Mela ground? And how did he know to order the food in the morning? . . .

LAWFULNESS OF THE UNIVERSE

It turns out that the universe is lawful—not in a logical law, by the way. The law I'm talking about is what would be called the divine law. That is, it's not logical law in the sense that a is a and not b. It's the law that includes paradox and all possibility. Within that law of the universe, everything that is in form—whether it is on this physical plane or on any of the other planes I've been talking about—is all perfectly lawful. When we reduce it to our logical analogue, which is not an exact analogue but similar, we can think in deterministic frameworks. There is no free choice in the deterministic system. That is, if the laws are just running off, they are just running off, and the experience of free choice is merely another run-off of the law. And under those conditions the past, present, and future are all perfectly lawfully related to one another.

Because we are in time, we think that the future has not yet happened. But it's very much like being a character in a book, and you're on page 23 and you don't know what's going to happen on page 24, because you think you're the character in the book. But now imagine you're reading the book—well, you could turn over and find out what happened on page 24. Now imagine you wrote the book. You would already know what happened on page 24. Hinduism and all these dualistic religio-philosophic movements talk about "the One" or the "one guru," or *satguru*, or however you want to talk about it; Judaism says "The Lord is One," and Jesus says, "My father and I are one." When you go into these traditions, you see that when he has extricated himself from the attachment I've been

137

talking about—physical, subtle, and all these different vibrational frequency plays—then he and consciousness are the same thing. And of course since it is all interchangeable, there's only one of it. The way in which it keeps manifesting in form or in these different planes and coming down into clouds and then solids—and all this is perfectly *lawful*—you would say in effect, "He is the law." God is the law.

That's the way the word "God" finally comes in, which is a hard one for us. But you could say that's why the Jews were so interested in the law, and what the Ten Commandments were that Moses brought back. Because the universe of form is merely the lawful manifestation of this energy into patterns, and because it is all lawful—past, present, and future—all *are* already. Therefore when you are around this being, my guru you see that he is no more in the present than in the past or the future, and to him it's all equally available. Often when I'm sitting with him he would look at a being and later in just a little conversation when it just comes out for some karmic reason I don't fully understand, he'll say something about what's going to happen to that guy. In the Tibetan tradition there's like a lama who sends out postcards saying, "Next Thursday at 2 I'm leaving my body. I'm going to die. I hope you will come join me." And everybody gathers and at Thursday at 2 he turns around three times, he sits down, and he dies. You know that a fully conscious being always knows exactly the moment he's going to die, if he cared. When he is going to "drop his body" is what the expression is—and that really is what it is, dropping the body. It means dying to the physical plane. Ramana Maharshi, very beautiful, had cancer of the arm and he wouldn't have it treated and the devotees said, "Oh Bhagavan—God—take care of your body." And he said, "No, it's finished its work on this plane." They said, "Don't leave us; don't leave us." And he looked at them like he was bewildered, and he said, "Where can I go? Just because you're not going to see me on the plane you're addicted to, do you think I'm going anywhere?"

My experience with my guru over this time is that in five years he has slowly taken me over—which is a hard one for Westerners. Like my father asks me, "Are you getting married?"—because the woman I used to live with is in India with my guru, and he keeps calling her Mrs. Ram Dass. So I say, "I don't know; he hasn't told me yet." My father comes out of the tradition where you don't ask somebody else if you are going . . . "What do you mean, he hasn't told you?" he says. "Don't you make any decisions on your own?" And I say, "No." No. Now from our point of view we really think we lost something. In the Christian Bible it's called "Not my will, but Thy will, O Lord." Because once you understand—who thought that he was making the decision in the bus to turn right? Once you realize you are not who you thought you were anyway—how long do you want to play out the little melodrama that you think you're doing it all? And if you don't think you're doing it all, and it's still all lawful, you might as well just sit and listen to how it all came out. That's the "Not my, but Thy will." It's what is called *surrender*—which we find so horrible because when we think of the word "surrender" we think of one ego surrendering to another. But if you imagine just surrendering into the law or surrendering the illusion that you are the choice maker . . . The idea is, when you surrender, is the result chaos? Is Freud right? Is the whole idea right that who we are is a wild animal? Or is that just more of the program?

four

KARMA AND REINCARNATION

The two concepts that make it all come together—which the East has but the West unfortunately threw out of its religions in the Councils of Nicaea, Trent, and Constantinople—are the ideas of *karma* and *reincarnation*. And that, in effect, says who we are as separate entities: beings who keep incarnating. That is, taking on form in certain vibrational frequencies which we will call the physical plane. Taking birth, in order to work out, to run off certain kinds of attachments, to get finished with attachment. When you get finally finished with the attachment, the desires that keep making you be born again and again cease, and you become one with "the One." And that is the merging back into the One. From a Zen Buddhist point of view, once you are in the One, there's no one. Of course, you don't see the One; you only see the One if you're two. Once you are in the One it's non-dualism.

Those two models, those two concepts, make an entirely different matter out of what the meaning of what your daily life is about, or what the meaning of human suffering is. Because once I see me as somebody who has taken on this package in order to carry out certain works of purification, I start to look at the experiences I'm having in life as part of that purification exercise. Then I see this life as a certain necessary kind of work that I am doing. It's the question of what is the meaning of life. But in order to do that, I am no longer using the basic philosophical foundation of the West, which is philosophical materialism. I don't mean materialism in the sense of I want to build a wristwatch. I mean materialism that says we are our human bodies, and when they're gone, baby, that's it; so get what you can now, because when it's over, it's done. When you look at the world from the viewpoint of philosophical materialism, and you look at the caste system that existed way back in India that's just coming to a decaying end now, you see horrible injustice. When you look at it from the point of view of incarnation, you see it in an entirely different way. In the villages in India, these people are still living "in the spirit." They are now identified with this earth in that way.

Now we in psychology call that a dissociative process, as a defense mechanism to protect one from undue anxiety. I mean, I know that game, too. That's one way of looking at it. That's the way to preserve philosophical materialism, which is a set of assumptions. But when you're working out of a different experiential base, philosophic materialism doesn't seem so valid to you. And once you get into another space, you see that you, in fact, have taken this birth for a certain function and you're just running it off. In those cases the king is doing his *dharma* or his perfect route, in which *his* thing is to be the perfect king; and the sweeper is doing *his* thing, which is to be the perfect sweeper. In the village the sweeper doesn't wish he were king, because the wish to be king is making him other than a perfect sweeper and his work is to run that one through. The king will be the sweeper, and the sweeper will be the king, and so on. Now, from our point of view, you say, "Oh, well, that's all fantasy and projection." But for people who are living in a different space or a different identity with themselves . . . Like the guy that I am talking about that I visited in India. He's in a village where you run down the street and say, "You know what Maharaj-ji just did? He told me this. . . ." And they say, "Oh sure, of course . . . but did you hear . . ." You know, to them it's common fare. In the village I live in everybody says, "Of course that stuff all happens. Nothing big deal about that." Because they are living much closer than we are to the space where all this is possible. For us it's called "miracle" because it doesn't fit in with our existing philosophical conceptual system.

Now, reincarnation doesn't have to be linear in the sense of the Bridey Murphy kind of thing. It may well be in terms of past, present, and future all being here simultaneously. There are many ways of thinking of the fifth dimension of infinite repetition and changes and so on. Many ways of thinking of reincarnation. I used to do personality research and we would try to predict when a mother and father did a certain thing, how the child would be in terms of Freud's identification theory. We were studying resistance to temptation, guilt, internalization of values, and sexual role identity: the four things that are supposedly the manifestation of identification. We would question the parents for many hours. We'd study the child with exquisite instruments, and we'd throw this all into a fantastically complex factor analytic design and we'd usually come out with a correlation, say between 40 and 60. A correlation of .4 means that you've accounted for 16 percent of the variability, which means that 84 percent of the variability hasn't been accounted for. Now we in social science say, "Well, if we could put more variables into the computer . . . it's just that it's such a multivaried thing . . . we can't predict it from a single variant." Or we say, "Well, we don't have the theory quite right—but almost. And when we do, it will go way up." But you see that 84 percent that's left we call random error. Or say that we haven't put variables into the machine: that very easily could allow for a number of different possibilities about how it all really is.

I don't question at all that my body is related to my heredity through my parental strain, and that my personality is affected by the internalization of values through my relations to my parents and society—my socialization. I don't question that at all. That is the package as far as I am concerned, but that isn't *who I am*. And in effect, from the reincarnation point of view, a person before birth knows exactly what they're buying into. It's not a pig in a poke; they know just what they're buying into. They say, "I'm buying into these parents, this experience. I'm going to be in this life, I'm going to have one eye, I'm going to be a cripple, I'm going to end up being beaten to death on the street in Benares and that's what I need. O.K., here I go." You dive down in, and the veil is lowered. There you are, and here we are, and we run through this one, and then we get all finished and we come back out of it and we wake up. O.K., you ran that one off; now let's see what's next. What I need to be now is a duke, and I might have to wait thousands of years for that one.

I know I'm pushing you very hard, but I'm just trying to give you a feeling. The game is much more interesting than we thought it was. You begin to see this entire physical plane as a training school. The minute you stop treating all of the experiences that every single being has had which don't fit in with your conceptual model of who you are and how it works as hallucinations or irrationality or psychosis or deviance, you understand it as, really, information. . . . You see, this is the issue: you go from being a decider, a judge. The judge says, "Will I accept what he is saying or not? He's a very persuasive fellow, but obviously he's taken too many drugs. He's left the realm of . . ." I mean, there's a judging place in all of us. And we are running all these experiences through our logical, rational mind, because we think that's a real big deal. From another point of view, as I've told you, there are obviously other ways of knowing. That is considered a *siddhi*, a power. Knowing through the intellect is merely another power. It's like prehensile hands was a big deal earlier, and then cerebral cognizing is another big deal.

In India, in the yogic tradition, they say, "Look, each thing seems like a big deal, but don't get hooked on it." Instead of saying, "Well, that's a good one—I'm going to use it and control . . ." See, we're interested in control and mastery. We can go to the moon, aren't we great? I can say it, but maybe you can't hear it; I can say from Maharaj-jis point of view, he *is* the moon. What does he want to go there for? What man has continually done, he's taken each little tool he's been given and used it in order to enhance the power of his own separate entitiness. In fact there is a whole other level where you become part of the process of it all, because you decide your own separate entitiness is merely part of a running-off process. You no longer identify yourself as a separate entity. The Chinese philosophy that is most in harmony with that is called *Tao*. It's given in a little tiny book called *Tao Te Ching*, which is probably from the philosopher Lao-tzu. It's just a statement of what the flow is, what the natural law is like. You become more and more like a river. When a river floats down the stream it doesn't say, I must follow the laws of gravity, or, today I think I'll float down the stream. There is no overlay of self-consciousness. We are under the impression that that overlay is what is our saving thing, while actually it turns out it's our losing thing, not our saving thing. It's a short-term gain and a long-term loss.

The funny thing about my journey at the moment is—the further I go, the less I think. The *Tao* says the student learns, by daily increment, the Way—meaning The Way, as when Christ says, "I am the way." The route, the harmony, is gained by daily loss: loss upon loss until at last comes the Way. When I talk to you about bringing your mind to one-pointedness, for example that time I'm sitting sixteen hours a day following my breath, think of all the books I could be reading, all the knowledge I could be collecting. Is it possible that by bringing my mind to one point I will know all that without knowing I know it but have it available to me? It's like what you're moving toward is the ideal computer program, which is not a fixed program. It's a totally fluid program. It optimizes all the data that is fed into it in terms of what function is necessary. That would be the ideal program. The program with no program. It's the program that is perfectly in harmony always with the optimum thing.

We think that if we don't think it's all going to go to hell.

What's far out is that you go through a period when you expect it's going to and when it seems to. That's where we need moratoriums at times when we are shifting programs. Then you come into a place where you think less and less, and more and more happens, and it gets more and more on base brain. It's a bad way of saying it, but roughly that's it. You are empty more and more of the time, and more and more of the time the perfect thing is happening all the time.

I used to do therapy, and a patient would come in and I had a model of what I thought patients were about. "I'm the doctor; you're a patient." I was a Freudian. I'd been trained in the psychoanalytic institute. I had a model about what psychosexual stages were. I had a whole set of models. The person would say "Bzzz" and that would go into this category in my head and I would say, "Oh, yes." Under Category A I would give Response 3. Now I didn't have it that exact, but it was that kind of a dance. They'd say, "My mother bzzz," and I'd write it down, and they could learn when to get the pellet. I mean, we have all seen those research studies showing how each therapist trains his patient to be Rogerian or Freudian, or whatever. Then he says, "You're cured," when the patient thinks like the therapist does.

Now imagine that you don't have any model at all in your mind about anything. You don't even have a model that there is a patient or that you are a doctor. Here's an entity that you happen to meet. You could meet him in a bus, you could meet him in bed, you could meet him in the office. Who knows where you are going to meet the next entity? Here we are. And who are we? Who do I see when I look at another human being? Am I focused? Which level is my microscope focused at? Do I see body? Well, if my sexual desires are what I'm attached to, that is what I will see. A beautiful entity goes by and I'll go "umm." And you know, yourself, when you walk down the street and you're horny or you're sexually lustful, that's all you see. You go by a bakery and you never even notice it. But if you are hungry you notice the bakery and the beautiful whatever-it-is doesn't do a thing to you . . . unless it has a roll in its hand. That's the predicament: your desires, your motives, affect your perceptions, as we all know. Now let's say you sit and you've trained yourself through the course of your understanding and your own discipline. All the desires are around, I mean, it's all functioning, but it's almost like your oil gauge in your car: when it needs oil, a red light goes on and you give it oil; but you don't have to be your oil gauge. The oil gauge is just doing its thing; the gas thing is doing its thing; everything is doing its thing, and you're just here. When I look at another person, I see body and then I see personality or hear personality or see that level. Tune a little deeper, there's personality. Now tune once more, and here we are. Here we are *sitting*. It's like you're sitting inside that package and I'm sitting inside this package. "You in there?" "Yeah, I'm here." But the way it comes out is through personality, and it comes out through body, and it comes out through the whole packaging process. The predicament is, do you define another human being as their package, or as their essence?

Now if you look through different levels of essence you can get essences which are still individual differences. There are astral differences, which is what astrology is about, as opposed to the MMPI, which is personality. Astrology is the MMPI of the next plane out. Like the Rorschach, you can keep looking, keep tuning, and go behind that one, behind that one, and behind that one till you come to the place where you are looking yourself in the eye. Because behind all individual differences there turns out to be only *one* of us. From my point of view at this moment there are, at the most, only two beings left in the universe. And much of the time there only seems to be One. But of the two that are left, one is who I still think I am, and God, or It All.

Everybody I meet is a teaching that has come to me. The reason I even see other beings is because of desires that I am still attached to, including this whole plane right here. The thing that collects us together is that we all have desires that involve this particular vibrational space. We all got born into this one, and, with very few exceptions, like the kind of guy I hang out with in India, most of us think that must be what reality is. It's like a group of people that are in a training school but who have never been outside the walls. It's like Plato's metaphor of the cave. All these beings are chained in the cave, and they have been chained so long that they have only seen the fire reflections on the opposite side of the cave, and they build a whole culture about that. And then one of the guys gets free at one moment and he goes out the door of the cave and he sees the sun and trees and all and he comes rushing back and he says, "Fellas, I hate to tell you, but . . ." and they stone him to death. That's what Plato points out. They stone him to death because they don't want to know. They don't want to upset the apple cart because it's too good. They're getting the payoff. They are getting the points. They are getting the reward. They are still attached to fulfilling their desires in time even though the relation of suffering and time hasn't dawned on them. That happens to people when they are getting ready to die. Then suddenly all their money and all their attachments and all their position and all the beauty all seems like so much, in Thurber's terms, "slish." It's just stuff. It's suddenly stuff and now they are going to face this thing and they don't understand. And for many of us, we saw the "slish" a little earlier than the moment before we are going to die.

What is happening in Western culture which is really awesome is that because of technology—not in spite of technology, because of technology—the limits of our rational mind are becoming more apparent sooner. And the limits of what we can take in terms of total fulfillment from the external world are becoming apparent earlier and earlier and earlier. A kid twelve years old has already vicariously run off, say, two hundred adult roles through television. He's already gone to the moon, he's already been a lawyer, he has already been the police chief of Los Angeles, he has already been a spy for the CIA. So you say, "What do you want to be when you grow up?" and the whole question is like an old-fashioned question, like, "What are you talking about?" He's gotten to the point where he is just right here now. He doesn't want to be anything. He's run out of them. He sees all those aren't what it's going to be either. He can look at the President and he can look at Frank Sinatra and he can look at all the boys that made it in the culture and say, "Oh-oh, boy . . . I don't want that—whatever that is, like that isn't quite right." And the sexual mores change so that he doesn't have to wait till he is thirty years old to have his first sexual experience. By the time he is fifteen he can often have finished the whole business. The game is changing, and the frequency of the use of marijuana and all this stuff means he is already playing with this loosening of his consciousness, and he has already been on other planes. So now, what is this being? Who is this? What happened? This is all out of technology, by the way. This is all out of the cultural philosophy of "More Is Better." We have collected more and more, and more and more, and the dawning thing is that more is never enough.

Despair is what motivates the next step. That is what we are talking about now. When man finishes being totally enamored of his power, of his intellect, and he can buy or control or master or get anything he wants and still . . . this is the "world of the gods." I can be a god and still be Ram Dass, or Richard Alpert, or whoever I was. I can know it and control it and can master it. Then comes the dawning thing—that it is all ephemeral. It's all ephemeral, and it isn't enough even when we get it. We've had wise men and sages—not so much in the West—but we have had beings who were totally fulfilled beings, and they have a certain vibrational space, and when you are around them you feel great peace. Certainly if great peace was contingent on the acquiring of things, we would expect the most beautiful, the most powerful, and the most successful beings in society to show that great peace. Well, usually they are an example of the people who least show it. Then, there comes a despair which is an absolute prerequisite for the whole trip: the despair that knows that how you thought you would make it isn't going to make it. That despair is a prerequisite to turn back inward, and turning back inward starts you to go for the next level, and that is roughly what many of us are now doing. Some of us do it in our spare time; some of us do it on Sunday morning or Saturday night; some of us try to build it into our work; some of us say, "Well, I can do nothing but just go the whole trip and see what happens."

It's very extraordinary for me as a psychologist to have let loose of so many models of how I thought it had to be. When a person walks in and sits down with me now, they come and they say, "My problem is brrr . . . and I'm suffering . . ." They get all done, and I'm looking right into their eyes—because the eyes are the windows of the soul—and I'm looking right through all that stuff. When they get all done, I say, "Right. I hear all that, and here we are. You're telling me about your melodrama, but that isn't who you are. 'Cause I can see, it's just stuff. It's like you are telling me about the paint job on your new Cadillac convertible." I really see therapy, in terms of personality, as body and repair work. But it has nothing to do with essence. Essence means that the therapist has to know who he or she is, because the therapy will be just as high as the therapist. A therapist who thinks he is a therapist can only create a patient who thinks he is a patient. A therapist who thinks he is a personality can merely exchange one personality package for another personality package. He can't even imagine that there is a way of being that has nothing to do with personality. Like, from a personality point of view a lot of my pathology isn't over. When I left analysis my analyst said, "You are too sick to function in society." That was in 1958, and he may well have been right. I've been just barely holding on ever since. The stuff is still around, but it is just stuff, just stuff, just stuff.

Now I will give you a little insight as to how I am playing this game. All this time I have been talking to you, all morning long, have I been identified with myself as the speaker? The far-out thing is, I'm not. I'm just sitting inside here and this whole thing is happening. I walked in here totally empty-minded; I had nothing I had to say to you. How am I going to collect points? Am I going to have you all say, "Very interesting"? Am I going to take it home and count it, put it in a scrapbook? "They were very appreciative down at . . . very wonderful"—big deal, so what? I'm doing this, 'cause this is what I do, 'cause this is what I do—like a shoemaker makes shoes. And what you get out of it is your current predicament. That has nothing to do with me. I'm doing this as my work on myself. I have no sense of social responsibility. None whatsoever, because that's just another attachment. I have no desire to do good. As I get freer of attachment, I *am* good. The Ten Commandments you can look at like, "Don't strike me dead." You can follow them out of fear, or you get to the point where you understand that they are describing how the universe works. And you, in effect, *become* the laws, the Ten Commandments. You don't follow them, you *are* them. Like, if I'm not attached to my separate body and personality, how can I steal from you? Who am I stealing from? I have to think, "I need something." It's like one hand stealing from another.

I have been having this interesting deal. This book, *Be Here Now*, has sold many, many copies and this community that did the art work and so on—they were the publishers—they got about 40 cents on every book. So suddenly they are sitting with $150,000 and money is corrupting them, and they are all getting . . . So I went to the distributor, and I said, "Look, let's change the whole game and reduce the price, and everybody cut out profit. . . ." So I'm working out to arrange to reduce the price, and I go to my father who is a very wealthy Republican from Boston with a big estate, and he says to me, "Well, what are you against, capitalism?" I said "No, I'm not against capitalism. I think it's wonderful. I'm happy you are a capitalist and you are enjoying it, and it's wonderful. I'm happy I do what I do and I don't want to change you. If there is more of you than me, then we have to play by your rules when we are in that certain space. If there is more of me than you, then you have to play by the other rules. That's the way the game is—you know, it's all a process." So he said, "I don't understand why you are cutting the price when it's a best seller. Everybody is willing to buy it. You could take the money and you could do good with it." I said, "Well, why can I do more good than the persons who put up the money? Tell me something—you're a lawyer—you just tried a case for your brother-in-law, didn't you?" "Yeah." I said, "Did you charge him a big fee?" "Of course not." "What did you charge him?" "I charged him my expenses." "Why didn't you charge him a big fee?" He says, "He's my brother-in-law." I said, "Well, that's my predicament. Everybody is my brother-in-law—what am I going to do?"

The thinking mind is based on subject-object, so when you look at another human being including yourself, you see the other being as her or him, or them. When you are less and less attached to separateness, you experience it all more as us, or as one. Since the experience determines your action, you no longer can act in a way that's based on optimizing the position of the individual, because you see that is just accruing more problems. The only instructions that I function under now in the world are the instructions from my guru, which seem very simple and kind of Mickey Mouse from a Western, sophisticated point of view: to love everyone, and serve everyone, and remember God. Those are my instructions. But remembering God is all of this I've been talking about—that's what this is all about.

We may have a hard time with words like "God" and "the Spirit," but that's what these issues really revolve around. This is where finally these huge institutions like religion and science and philosophy start to find their way into the space where you are no longer attached to the More, or to the Separate. This is what is commonly known in the religious tradition as "living in the spirit." When you are living in the spirit it all looks different to you. Living in communion or harmony with your universe as man-in-nature, you see the thing that keeps you from living in the spirit all the time. The incredible thing is that the true power of the universe you can *be* but cannot have. When Christ said, "Had ye but faith, ye could move mountains," he was speaking literal truth. But were you able to move mountains, you wouldn't be you any more; you would be the Being who created the mountain in the first place. There is only one Being. And at some level equally as real as this physical plane, there is only one of us, and at another plane there aren't any of us.

My route is the route of the heart or of devotion. That is a path. There are many pathways through here. One is the path of wisdom, one is the path of calming the mind, one is the path of opening the heart. My path is the path of love.

Gurdjieff talks about three levels of love. There's physiological, biochemical love—"Let's make love." There is romantic love, which is personality love, loving an object, which has in it jealousy and hate and possession and all the psychodynamics of what we usually think of as personality and romantic poetry and so on. Then there is a third thing called conscious love. That is where you enter into the space which we previously called energy, and then consciousness. Another identity to those two identities is the word "love." Where you in effect become love: not "loving" as a verb, but "are love." A being around you experiences you vibrationally . . . when they are open. . . . When you say, "I fell in love with so and so, I'm in love with so and so," what you are really saying is, "They are a key stimulus which is an innate releasing mechanism to the place in me where I am love." And in effect when I live in the place where I am love, everybody I look at is my lover. So far out, as you can imagine. That doesn't demand you do anything about it. We're all right here in love. And when you meet another being, to the extent they are ready, they resonate right in that place; it's like a harmonic resonance. They resonate in the place where they are, in that place which is always ready in everybody but usually covered over with so much paranoia, where they also are love—not are loving, but are love. Suddenly here we are in the ocean of love which is what Christ's love was about. That love has no possessiveness. What am I going to collect—your body? Very scary. I'm going to collect you in time and space? I don't need to collect it, because I am it. Part of the illusion we are born into is a resultant internalization of negative "takes" which become part of our ego structure and which lead into a "take" of ourselves—which does not allow us to honor and taste of our own divinity, our own beauty, our own love, our own presence.

The minute you can look at another being and just focus right in on that place and let all the rest of the stuff be stuff—blowing by—then as fast as that person brings it up, it's gone. It's what is known as the "mirror phenomenon." A guru, or a conscious being, is a pure mirror for another being. It's not feeding back theory. It's just mirror. It's just empty. When I sit talking to you now, I am doing mantra. Inside, ever since I sat down here, has been going RAMMMM, RAMMMM. You see, my name is Ram Dass. Dass means servant; Ram is one of the incarnations of God. I am a servant of God—not my will, but Thy will. That name is a training device for me. My guru said, "Now you are no longer Richard Alpert, now you are Ram Dass." When he talks to me, he says "Ram Dass," then he says something to me; and I realize he is not talking to who I think I am, he is talking to who I would be, would I stop thinking I was somebody. And when I said to him, "It's going to be scary going back to America," he said, "You shouldn't fear anything." I said, "All I fear is my own impurities." Because, as I said, when you are sexy you see sex, when you are hungry you see food. You can only see your own impurities, anyway. The universe is the projection of your desires. So he came and he looked me up and down and he said, "I don't see any impurities." I thought, What, is he putting me on? And then I realized, No—from where he is looking, there aren't any.

We have been trained from the beginning in individual differences, and the reason we as an intellectual community are gathered together is because we are all masters at the game of individual differences. We can categorize, and analyze and compartmentalize better than practically anybody else in society. That's why we are sitting in this building at this moment. And it's great to have that as your servant. If that is your master, you're trapped. Behind it all, here "I" am. Here "we" are. Here "it" is.

ATTACHMENT

It always boils down to this question: How did we get so attached in the first place, or why? I have really nothing but a cop-out answer for that. I mean not a clear answer because, just as I said, ultimately the laws of the universe are not rationally knowable, because they are not within the logical rational system, since that is a subsystem, and there is a meta-system of which that's all part, which includes paradox and opposites. Almost every religion ultimately says, "That question cannot be asked or answered." Like in Judaism there is a statement "In the beginning," and they say that of all the things the Talmudic scholar can study—the scholar of Torah—that is the one thing that a teacher cannot teach him, nor can a book help him with. He can only know that through meditation you go inward to the place where you *are* the answer, but you don't know the answer. In other words, Buddha's answer in very gross terms is "It's none of our business"—our business in the sense of the person who asks and answers questions.

I can give you hundreds of answers that have been given by religions around the world to that question. Why did it all begin? Why is there suffering? Why did it go from the zero into the one into the many? You know, in some systems it is cyclical. It's just going, and going, going, from the zero to the one to the many, back to the one, back to the zero, and on and on and on and on. From another place, nothing is happening, because it is all still in time. And a few levels out you are not in time any more, and then it always has been and it always was and it always will be, and nothing has happened yet. I mean there are so many game levels to answer that from, and my answer is that at the level I am at, I just don't know. I don't know. It doesn't mean it isn't knowable; it's just that I don't know it.

It's always the question you are finally forced to: So why did it all begin? What's it all about? It's just like the meaning of suffering. There is a certain stage . . . where you are trying to avoid suffering, and you are afraid of death. So your whole philosophy in life is built on the fear of suffering and the fear of death. Then you get to a place where you have seen a little more, and you are not so afraid of death. You're sort of mildly curious about it. Then you get to a place where you start to see that suffering is purification: it's like the fire that gets you straight. It's like a prerequisite for this work. And then at that point suffering takes on a whole new meaning for you and you have a whole new way of looking at the universe. Like I was just with this boy, twenty-three years old, who was dying of Hodgkin's disease out in California, and he and I were talking about his impending death and preparation for it. Very calm, right here. I could see that the people around him were saying, "Isn't it terrible that a person so young should die?" But I don't feel that at all. My feeling is, how do I know when a person has finished his work? I don't know what his work is. It would only be my fear of death that would make me want to keep that person alive, longer and longer and longer. Otherwise I would just want to hear how it came out. I'm not attached.

Imagine that this is a training program, a training school— and it's not even a very exciting training school, it's one of the lower-level ones. Suppose a person has very little to do, and they can do it in about three years. So they come and they do it in three years, and at the end of three years they start to die of meningitis or whooping cough. And we say, "What kind of God could that be, that is taking that child from us now?" Well, that person, that being, has finished its work. That's a whole different philosophical place from the place at which the person is moaning. Job in the Bible is a perfect example of this. "What are you doing to me, God?" God in effect could have answered, "Because you are my chosen." You're my chosen. Because suffering purifies. You get to the point like, when I suffer, I don't choose to suffer—I'm not a masochist—but when I suffer, I am working with it rather than suffering. I am seeing the suffering. And as this philosophical position keeps changing, as you keep evolving in these positions, the answer to that question you ask keeps changing and the reason for asking the question keeps changing. At one point it's a burden, then the next moment it's a joy, then the next moment it's nothing.

How Do We Know?

There are three ways in which you know things. One is you know them through direct experience. One is you know them because somebody you know knows them, and tells you. And one of them is you study them with your logical mind which extrapolates outward. My predicament is that there have been many, many experiences that I've had which are not conceptually organized—they are all like pieces of puzzles that are all hanging around. Then when I read something, or I'm with somebody whom I trust, like this being I know in India, and he says something, because of the little pieces of puzzle in my being, what he says has an inner validity to me that says, "Yeah, right on." While somebody else that doesn't have those little pieces of puzzle would say, "Well, I don't know; that's just his position." You see? And in a way, a lot of what I know about all this stuff comes through being around these kinds of beings and through my readings of what are called the sacred books of the world, which are descriptions by various mystics and saints of the states and the work on other planes of consciousness, which comes through things like Theosophists and the Buddhist tradition and the Christian mystics like John and Theresa and so on, the Eastern mystics, Eastern Greek Orthodox Christians, the Sufi tradition, the mystics of Moslem tradition, and a lot of Egyptian writings which are concerned with things like this, with the preparation and training of sages, and higher and higher planes. But when I read this stuff— some of it, I read and it just goes by me, 'cause it's not relevant, I'm not ready for it, or I don't have the pieces of the puzzle to make it fit together. But other stuff, "Yeah, right on."

There are certain attachments that an individual has which can only be worked out or realized on the physical plane. That is, they have to actually take a physical birth to work through that attachment. Working through an attachment means you have to work with that desire until you are no longer attached to that desire. The desire may go on, but you are not attached to it. Some work can be done on other planes, which are different vibrational spaces where beings have other kinds of qualities to them. That is, there are certain planes where beings can take on bodies at will—whatever body they need for certain work. There are bodies made of light; there are all these different astral planes. Some of it is described, for example, in books like Yogananda's book, *Autobiography of a Yogi*. A lot of the Theosophists have described these. Leadbeater has an exquisite description of these different planes. What generally happens to an individual depends on where his consciousness is at the moment of death. At the moment of death, if the person is holding to life—versus Gandhi for example . . . the moment he's shot . . . Probably when somebody is shot they go "Umph!" or "Don't blame them," or "Goodbye," or something. Gandhi is shot—he comes out of his back yard and he is shot with four bullets—and as he is toppling over he says, "Ram," the name of God. He just goes out, right?

He's so ready to go, he's got his bag packed and by the door. He's just come out to give a press conference—but he is so ready to go that he gets shot and he doesn't say, "I should remember Ram"—he just goes, "Ram." Well, now that kind of being is in a different predicament when he drops his body than another being who thought he was his body. Because most beings who thought they were their body, when they die they enter into a space which is called purgatory in Christianity. It's kind of a floating in space, full of confusion—utter confusion. Because you can't imagine that you are still around and that you aren't who you thought you were. You haven't been prepared with a lecture like this, you know, to say, "Oh, right, that's what that was about." See, I mean you are not in that position. There is a horror to that moment—it's just absolute, total, confused panic.

The Tibetan Buddhist's preparation for people dying is very interesting, because that describes seven planes. Seven turns out to be a very hip number in the melodrama. What they say to the person they are preparing for death is, "When you go out, the first thing you are going to experience, the first place you are going to be, is this—if you are free enough to be able to be in that space, which is where you don't exist any more. It's just merging . . . that's *it*—you've done it; you are finished." If on the other hand you blow that one, because you are too confused or too frightened or you're holding on to it too much, you then come into the next plane. If you are too frightened and it's too much for you, you come into the next plane. Try to stay there. If you can't make it there, you come into this one. And they bring you down through seven planes, and finally the one where you take rebirth, on this plane. And they prepare you for all these different planes. Just like when a Japanese person is dying—if they know they are going to die, they put a screen in front of them which has Buddha and the pure land. It's like a ticket, like a railway ticket to the next place. They say, "O.K., you are ready to go—this is where you are going to go. Just keep it in mind, and whatever you see on the way through, don't stop, don't buy from beggars off the street—just keep going." Now, the only beggars off the street, you see, are desires you still have.

What in effect is happening is that most of the desires we have do not need physical bodies to be satisfied; only a few of them do. There are many that are satisfied in much more subtle bodies: thought and feeling levels, feelings of love, desires to be loved, things like that. To be separate and loved—that one is a really deep one. Well, you could sit and be separate and loved without a body on the astral plane like for about 500,000 years. But time is a different concept in those spaces than in this. When you finish this plane, you look at this whole thing, and sixty years seems like that (snaps fingers). It's almost like you decided, "Well, I think I will think about this for an hour. O.K., that was interesting." But even when you are in the middle of it, it seems like it's as long as it is, but you notice as you get older how it goes faster and faster. You are getting into a different space regarding time, and from one level out this whole thing is like that (snaps fingers), or eternal, depending on how far in you get. Nirvana—the place between the seventeen trillion mind moments—is eternal. You can be there for eternity.

There is a kind of a horrible, beautiful description in a book by Ruth Montgomery about a fellow by the name of Ford. Ford was a medium, and he died and then he used Ruth Montgomery to type out some reports from the other side. Now most of us in Western science, we treat that stuff like, you know, pretty mushy, soft stuff. But from where I am looking at it, it's all straight, that's all real communication, it's really happening. But Ford himself had many desires. And so he is living in a realm created by his desires. See, as you get farther out you become more conscious that mind creates matter, and you see that you keep creating the universe around you, just as I said when you are hungry you walk down the street and bakeries are suddenly the dominant thing, and grocery stores, while otherwise you walk down and you don't even notice they exist. Your desires *create* your universe. Well, it becomes more and more apparent on these astral planes. What we call heaven, which turns out to be hell, also—the United States is getting more like that all the time—is a space where you can get whatever you want. And then it isn't enough, of course, but you can get whatever you want. The gods can have whatever they want. But whatever you can have and want isn't what it all is, except the final peace, and that doesn't come from getting it, but from being it. You can't "get" peace, just like you can't "get" wisdom, but you can be wise. You can "get" knowledge but you can only *be* wise—those are two different spaces entirely.

So most beings go through a very confusing period, and then, in effect, they are guided or trained in the same way that we are being guided and trained; but most of us don't realize we are being guided. The awakening is to the realization that you are in fact being guided. That's why I say there are only two of us, for me. There's me and God. The whole dance of my life is the training in which the universe is teaching me things which are bringing me toward the One. It's like the guru has me on a hook, like a trout, and he's just bringing me in—slowly—and I'm going through all these different experiences while I think I'm rushing this way and rushing that way. But slowly the thing is being brought in and everything that's happening to me is part of my liberation.

Almost all saints say, when you finally see, you see it all for the good. Like a doctor just came up to me and he said, "If these saints are all so high, why don't they relieve human suffering instead of sitting around? Why don't they do something?" And I say, "Well, you've got to understand what they understand before you can ask why they do what they do. To relieve one kind of suffering is increasing human illusion. You have got to understand. You can't judge another person till you know what they know. Because they may know more than you know about why it is that way. All you can do is purify yourself, instead of judging others."

Beings only go through that confusion state if they are not prepared. If they are prepared, they immediately go to where their next work is, whatever plane it is. That is, a person that is fully prepared will go out and immediately may take another birth—right away. Somebody else may wallow in this place for a long time until they are guided into some other space where they have their next work to do, and then they do that for another lifetime and another plane, and then they might come back to a human birth. They may go through these dances. There are other beings who don't have to take births any more. They are just running through a very subtle kind of karmic process, running off on planes of pure thought. They aren't even manifest in forms at all, nor emotion. That's Plato's Absolute: the idea of Pure Idea.

The thing is that you can tune yourself. Various saints tune to different planes and they meet various beings—like some people meet poltergeists and ghosts. Those are beings on very low planes, some of whom are still confused and trying to get back into a physical body. They are trying to take people over, and trying to possess people and all the stuff that we call possession. But you can only be possessed if you have desires of your own. That is, if you want power. Somebody comes along and says, "Look, I will give you power, the power of being somebody outside of the physical body, if you will let me use your body." There is all this weird stuff that goes on, which somebody that is pure and seeking for God never even notices. That's all irrelevant. It's just like you walk down the street and there are a lot of pickpockets, hustlers, and all that; but if you are going somewhere you don't even notice them. They are just all beings, and you don't get caught in them. While if you're looking to hustle somebody, you suddenly notice all the other hustlers around. It's like my teacher used to say to me, "You know, when a pickpocket meets a saint, all he sees are his pockets. He never even sees the saint."

All these different beings on these lower planes are just like us, except they don't have a physical body. That's really what it boils down to. Now then, there are these higher places which in the literature are called heavens; the lower ones are called hells. These are our labels for these different vibrational spaces where beings are doing different kinds of work. Through your meditation or a certain mantra you may tune to a certain plane where you meet a being who is "The Lord in Heaven" and you say, "Wow, I've met the Lord in Heaven!" The Lord in

Heaven is just another being who is running off its karma on that plane. It happens to be the Lord of Heaven—that round. Just like you might go to the White House and meet Nixon, who is the Lord of Earth or whatever you want to call that. I mean, it's the same sort of trip. All the heavens and hells, they are all just more of these planes. Behind all of that is Thought or Law, and behind all that *isn't*. Or Is, but unmanifest. There is unmanifest and manifest and it's all right here now. It's all right here. It's not there. It's all here. There are some beings who are on higher planes, and then they choose to take a human birth because their work on that higher plane involves some run-off that can be best done on this plane. But it's not like we do it—where we go unconsciously into the birth. They consciously do it—like Christ, like Jesus.

Jesus is the son of God in the sense that it's an astral being who takes a physical form in order to do a certain kind of work. What blows our mind is things like the Immaculate Conception and all that stuff—like how could that be? How could somebody go without water or food? We don't understand it. We can't handle any of that stuff, so we say, "Well, it's just lousy reporting; that's really what it boils down to." When, in fact, beings from these planes do manifest; what we call a guru like the man I deal with who is called a guru, who is sitting with a blanket in India—that's a doorway. But that isn't *who he is*. When I go through that one, through my meditation, I meet another being who may not be shaped that way; he may just be a certain feeling or presence: that's another doorway. And each one of these—it's like Chinese boxes, you just keep opening this and there is another one—you open this and there's another one—you open this and there's another one and when you finally open the last one—there you are. That's far out—there you are.

And so the guru is merely another method, and you don't get hung up on the guru on the physical plane, because that's another trip. That's just like meditation or mantra or chanting, or anything else. Just another trip. And he knows he isn't that.

163

Well, he doesn't really know anything. You're busy rubbing the feet of this thing, and you suddenly realize you are like rubbing the feet of a dog. He couldn't care less if you rub his feet or not, and all the time he is saying, "Oh, it's so wonderful to have you rub my feet." And you're feeling, Aren't I good to be rubbing his feet? Then you suddenly think, I've been had—how do you like that? He took me again. So you go and you sit down. You just go in and you're empty, and you just focus here on the guru, and suddenly you meet him in another place and you get all razzle-dazzled—and you've met him on the astral plane, and it's all groovy—and then suddenly you realize you've been had again. Your fascination and your excitement and bliss and all make you cling to these planes. Most beings cling to one plane or another. So when they die they just land on one plane or another, still clinging, doing their work. A fully conscious being when he leaves his body, leaves his body the same way that you'll take your next breath. With no more melodrama than that. And when they leave their body, that's it. They just —they leave—they're just done.

So part of our work is working with dying people. That's why my major reflections these days have been concerned with the development of a center for dying. That is, a place where beings in this culture could come to die consciously: to be surrounded by people who themselves are not afraid of dying, and who will provide an environment for them where there isn't a total denial of death and only other people who are afraid of dying. What it's coming to now is a service for people, including training seminars for the families of those that are dying, to get them ready to be with the person consciously at the time of death—and an exploration of various kinds of anesthetics to relieve pain but not wipe out consciousness, so the person can be very conscious just at the moment. Because the training for dying is exactly what the training for living is. It's a training to be right here now—"Now right here"—"Now right here." Like Aldous Huxley when he died. He took LSD. His wife gave him LSD and he sat and he said, "Now I don't feel any more feelings in my legs . . . now I don't feel any more feelings in my thighs . . . the thigh is gone . . ." and things like that. He just slowly left his body—just mildly curious. That's the intellectual trap. So he'll have another million years in a place where he can satisfy all his curiosity. Just another subtle one. Because ultimately you are not even curious—you're just taking the next breath, which is what all of us should be doing now. Every moment is our moment of birth and our moment of death, and here we are, and O.K.—now what? Now what? And now what? That's the optimum way for that transformation. It's just a transformation of energy. Nothing more or less than that.

But if you think you are more than energy, you're going to be frightened. Because you think you've got something to lose. That's why I think the LSD research here in this place is really one of the major breakthroughs in this culture. As far as I am concerned, this is allowing people to psychologically die prior to physical death, which gives them a chance to experience the dissolution of ego, up to a certain point. The thing is that with a drug you are overriding desire. Those desires stay in subtle forms, and those subtle forms determine the future incarnation. So you are not shortening the trip, you are merely optimizing the use of this life. But, you know, in a way you are going through it—it's your karma to be in this Center and be a terminal cancer patient and be dying here—I mean that's your karmic predicament.

You can't actually rip away an attachment, because that's an attachment too. Attachments fall away like a snake molts its skin—that's really much more of an apt analogy. But what you feel, you experience, your doing—is just the subjective experience that you are doing anything since there is actually no doer doing anything. The subjective experience of doing something is that you confront some desire. A certain amount of wisdom makes you see that you aren't that desire. And wisdom starts to dislodge it just a little bit. Meditation, or bringing the mind to one point, dislodges it a little more, because for moments you are free of it.

Now, there are various strategies for how to work with a desire. One is not to do the thing that the desire is connected with. Like my guru put a cup of tea in front of me, and said to me, "Do you want it?" I'd say, "Yeah." He'd say, "Then don't drink it." Now, that's a very fierce strategy. See, the predicament is that you might spend the next five hours wanting that cup of tea. That's what celibacy usually is in the church. They are busy not having sex. "I cannot have sex for another day. I know I can get through it. I'm not going to think of sex. . . ." You can't *not* think of a rhinoceros the minute somebody tells you "Don't think about a rhinoceros." You can try to stop something prematurely, but in a way you are just feeding it. You are feeding the reality of it by the preoccupation. So the optimum strategy under those conditions seems to be to do whatever the thing is, but remain as much as possible in the state of the *witness*—which in defense mechanism terms would be called dissociation. But it isn't dissociation out of anxiety. It's dissociation out of growth. So it isn't a defense mechanism. It's—you take on a place. You find the "I" in you.

I used to be obsessed with root beer. You see, I have things like root beer and pizza—which you know are just not yoga food. So I sit up in my room and I say, "O.K., I'm just going to sit," and it's so beautiful. And suddenly the next moment I'd be at the refrigerator and I'd have a bottle of root beer tilted back and I'd be drinking it. Then the first thing I'd say is, "Damn it, I broke down again—I'm no good." And then another voice within me would say, "Drinking root beer—and putting himself down for drinking root beer." In other words there was another voice in me which has no judgment—it couldn't care less whether I drink root beer or not—it's merely noticing what is going on. It's a completely dispassionate witness—not a judge. It's not the superego. It's not saying, "You'll never make a good yogi because you're bad." It's saying, "There you are—there's that and there's that and there's that." Well, what happens in the course of the development of this wisdom is that you are spending more and more time being that part of yourself, rather than the rest of it. So you say, "Ah—there's the desire to achieve, or there's the desire for power, or there's that desire, or there's that one running off. It's like a subliminal flicker thing. You're doing something out of a desire that's taking you over, and then there's a moment when you see what you are doing—which is usually followed by a judgmental moment. But then you witness the judgment, and you keep going through these little flickering things with the desires that you're not ready to stop because there's too much force in them still.

DEEPEST DESIRES CONNECTED
WITH SURVIVAL AND REPRODUCTION

Certain desires have more force than others. Ones that are connected with survival and reproduction of the species obviously are going to have the most built into them—like sex and food and so on. They are really deep and powerful, but you develop more and more of this Witness, just like subliminal information stuff. First it comes in once every ten units—a moment where you just see it. Then it's two out of ten, till pretty soon it's there more and more times. Just like today, I am resting inside watching this speaking and watching this listening, not particularly being identified with the speaker or with the listeners. There is just this process going on, and I'm watching it. Like if somebody comes in and he sits down and he looks like he's thinking, Well, I'll listen to him, but I won't believe it—you know, that's a very reasonable thing in a place like this. Then you see that something happens—the mouth softens just a little bit, see, "Oh, that's interesting"—and then later on you see a smile. Now, to the extent that there is ego in you, you can say, "See, watch. (Snaps fingers) Look—got another one." But when I see that, and when I see that reaction in me, I see both of those things

167

and I say, "Yeah, right, that's the way the universe is. That's nature, running off."

There is still a place in this personality that wants to be loved. It isn't who I am, but this personality has its own independent life; it's doing its trip. Well, slowly you become more and more of the witness, and as you are doing that you are feeding these things less and less. It's like if you ever tried to make love and stayed conscious through the whole act of making love—which is what tantric sexuality is about . . . you'll find it is really quite difficult if not impossible for almost everybody, because you get lost into being the experiencer of the sensual pleasure; and as you get lost in the experience, you've lost the witness.

There is a Buddhist meditation for eating, which is really far out. You put food in front of you, and when you reach for the spoon, you say, "Reaching, reaching." You say each thing twice: "Lifting, lifting; placing, placing." You're saying this to yourself. "Chewing, chewing; tasting, tasting; savoring, savoring; swallowing, swallowing; digesting, digesting; reaching, reaching; lifting, lifting." By the time you are halfway through the meal you've got the screaming meemies. The enjoyer of the food has been destroyed by that. Now if you try doing that for about a year, the whole meaning of going to a meal changes considerably, I'll tell you. Because you have become the witness of the whole process rather than the enjoyer of it. Right?

You can't rip yourself from being the enjoyer prematurely, but there is a point where it starts to fall away. For most of us, we invest in something that we enjoy, and when it starts to fall away we get upset, because we previously thought it was something. Like I worked hard to get my pilot's license, in order to buy an airplane. Then I get to the point where you just go up for four hours and then you go straight—you come down, you go to the toilet—you get a milk shake—you fill up with gas—you sit for four hours—you come down. Big deal. So who needs that? But I paid $7,000 for the plane and it's taken me hundreds of hours to get my license. And it takes me a long time before I can afford to realize that I have used up the thing. The thing is that we keep using up things but we can't let them go. When we have another way of looking at it, we're really ready to let go very quickly of a lot of them. But others, we still think we are going to get our rush from them, see, particularly ones like sex and eating and stuff like that. To bring those under consciousness you can only edge up on them—sort of around the corner with a little bit of witnessing, you know—that's the way you deal with desires. Then as they are ready, and as your wisdom gets great and your mind gets calmer and your purification gets deeper, it falls away—it keeps falling away and falling away and falling away.

For example, I told you my own instructions at this moment are love, serve, and remember. I don't have any form in that, and part of my work—as a training procedure for myself—is to stay as light as possible. I float around now—I float around the country, I float around the world, I have no form, I have nothing I have to do. It's very hard to be free-floating. It's like free-falling parachute jumping. You keep wanting to cling to somewhere—like "Well, I'll have a schedule, a lecture schedule," or "I've got to do good," or "I'm known—I can use that force, that power to do bzzz"—and everybody comes and plays upon that thing. They say, "Well, don't you want this, or don't you want that?" The game is just to stay in totally free fall, and do whatever you do, like this is what I'm doing—you know, Lock said, "Come down and speak," and so here we are. Because that was a message, not because I am hoping. I don't have any model of why I am doing this or anything else in my life. I'm not collecting anything. I don't have a goal. I'm just a pure instrument in the game.

Giving up the attachment to who you think you are and what you think you are doing is a really scary one. People say, "What do you do with your life?" "I don't know what I'm doing." "So who are you?" "I don't know who I am—who do you think I am?" See, like this group comes in, and the consciousness of this group sees a certain thing which elicits a certain thing out of me. Believe me, if I'm sitting with a group of young spiritual Westerners in the early morning fog at a beach, what comes out of me is a very different cup of tea than this thing. I don't plan that, but I notice when I hear tapes. I see that when I give a lecture at the Menninger Foundation it's entirely different than when I give a lecture to Hell's Angels or something like that. The content is the same, but the metaphor changes, because the metaphor is determined by the consciousness, even though I don't sit around and plan that. It just keeps happening.

Other Forms of Life

I think everything in form is running off karma, but I don't know what the units are. Like I don't know whether the rock is what it is, or whether the cells of the rock are what it is. Like I don't know which level the game is at in that sense. If you read Meher Baba you go through mineral, animal, vegetable, etc., and these are all part of reincarnations. I don't know that to be true. I've never experienced anything like that so I really don't know. But I think the reason a human birth is considered precious is because of the degree of *self*-consciousness—awareness of one's predicament. A cow very rarely knows that it's a cow, and a dog—even though a dog can show a great intelligence at times—has very little concept of itself as a dog, in relation. That seems to be a critical factor that's necessary for what is called the "awakening" in that birth. So I think that almost everything other than human birth is a mechanical running off of karma.

In the Indian system they talk about the three *gunas*, or three forces in the universe: *Tamasic, Rajasic* and *Sattvic,* or the force of inertia, the form of fire or energy, and the form of purity or the sattvic. Everything is a composite of these three forces. They would say a rock is primarily a Tamasic form, and fire is Rajasic, and beings are just going through these different forms. But that's a hard one; that's beyond me.

When you say, "I can't comprehend it," it's because the thinking mechanism you have works within time—so time and space are the matrices against which you think. The predicament of dimensions which are not linear—not linear time or linear space—where here and now are both here, and now and then are both now—those are ones we can't *think* about. That's the predicament. There is a book by Maurice Nicol called *Living Time*, which deals with this a great deal. I personally have had the experience—some of you have had this experience also—where I've looked at another being and seen their entire incarnation. I see the baby and I see the old man, I see the dying and I see the whole process—you can see the whole thing right in it. It's all right there, right at that moment. It's only because of your predicament in time that you think that you are relating to one part of it or another. Those are perceptual things that have happened to me. But I don't know much more about it than that. All I can say is that you just have to go a few levels out before time is totally irrelevant. Like when you listen to me. If you were to close your eyes and listen to me—without looking at this body—and I asked you to say how old I was, you'd find it very difficult because I don't think of myself as any age. I know this body is forty-one years old, but I am not a forty-one-year-old being. Sometimes when you'd listen to me you'd say it's a very old, old, old wise man, and sometimes you'd say it's a very little wise-guy child. It floats in and out of all these different aged beings, because I don't have any model of my age. That's why 99 percent of the people I hang out with are probably under twenty-five years old. I don't ever feel that I'm any different in age from them—nor do I think that they are particularly obsessed with the predicament either. Because of their interests they aren't in this age or time dimension that same way either: because one level out, you see that who you are isn't moving in time. Time is describing the incarnations, the packaging changes.

The desire to become enlightened is still you desiring something. What happens is you start to touch places way beyond what you ever thought you were. Or you start to awaken, and it's like the bliss is much more incredible, the understanding is more incredible, and so on, and the craving for it. It's like a supercrave and that desire is what is used to finish all the other desires. Then, near the end of that sequence, you're left with only that desire; and you see that the desire for it is what's keeping you from it. Then there's the having to let go of the desire in order to become it, which is the final process of dying, really. It's the psychological dying because desiring that last desire is your final statement of who you are. But the predicament is that who you are can't go through the doorway. You can get right up to the door and you can knock, but you can't go in. They say "it" can come in, but "you" can't. That which desires to get through the door gets right up to the door, and then they say, "The desire's gotta stay right out here. Sorry, leave your shoes outside, but you can come in." At that point the desire falls away. What has happened to me now—really interesting—although I still have plenty of other desires that are getting more and more subtle all the time—that desire is really much less than it ever used to be. It's like—to be as honest as I can—I don't know what birth I'm in, I don't know when it's over. There's nothing much I can do about it—I'm just living as consciously, and openly and trustingly as I am living and it's much more like "Here it is, and now what?" I can't even try to be conscious, because even trying to be conscious is unconscious. So there is no more trying, there is just being. Like, I've meditated because I've tried to meditate, but I could see that it was just another ego trip. Then finally I'd give it up, and then sometimes I'd be drawn into meditation. Meditation would happen to me. So much more now, my

172

life is happening *to* me—rather than I'm trying to make it happen.

That's a transformation in that sense. Less and less am I an experiencer of it—which is another part of the far-out thing, because we usually measure where we're at by the nature of the experiences we have. Like we get high or we feel the light, or we feel the presence of something, and we say, "Ah, wonderful." See, we got another mark, like, you know, "Good, I got another one—I just made another one." See? Then you get to the point where you see that the collecting of experiences —like the desire for enlightenment—is just another one of those things. That starts to go, until finally when an experience comes along, you just note it and just let go. Finally you are dead to worldly life, but you are fully alive, in the same way that water is. You are just doing your thing, but you are not busy collecting it. You are not experiencing it or collecting it, and in a way it's a horror show because you have died. I am sitting at my own dying and funeral. That's really what this process is that I am going through. I am surrendering into pure instrumentality. And the less I am, the more it is; the more optimum this thing is, the less I care about it; or, the less I'm trying to engineer it into being something else. . . . It's like Ramakrishna. You know, he loved the divine mother Kali so much that he kept craving to be with Kali and worship her. Finally his jungle guru said, "You've got to give up Kali." And he said, "Man, if I've got to give up Kali, I don't want to go." The guru took a rock—a pointed rock—and stuck it against his forehead and just kept pressing until Kali shattered into a million pieces in Ramakrishna's mind, and then he entered into the next space, which is beyond duality.

It's like if you have always wanted to have a lover that's the perfect lover, and you finally have the lover that's the perfect lover, it's really hard to merge with that lover—because then there's no more lover. No more lover and beloved. You give

173

up dualism, see. The experiencer, or the desirer, or the blisser is all in dualism. In that place beyond dualism—then you're nobody—and there's nothing. It's just pure instrumentality. That is what surrendering truly is, or "Not my, but Thy will," or the dying into service, or being an instrument of God, or however you want to say it. Then you leave it in the hands of God whether or not you are going to live or die, or serve or not serve, and you don't decide for yourself what's best.

index

175

Chusang Tsu, 19
Collective unconscious, the, 30, 90
Communal living (communes), 2–6, 48
Communication, 45, 47–48, 160
Compassion, 70, 72, 82, 88; without pity, 73–75
Competition, learning and, 98
Comprehension, 171–72
Computers, use of, 120–21, 132, 145
Confrontation, polarization and, 38–39
Consciousness, 1–6ff.; and attachment(s), 6–8, 85–89, 137ff. (*see also* specific kinds); Cayce and two states of, 55–57; centering and, 91–92 (*see also* Centering); chakras and (*see* Chakras); diet and food and, 65–68; distinctions between English and Sanskrit and, 92–93; drug use and (*see* Drugs, use of); "Eastern" and "Western" models of man and, 116–28; evolving, 6, 8, 25, 42, 46–47ff., 51, 53–54, 58, 76; fear and higher states of, 57–59; gnostic intermediary and, 81–82; group, modification of, 49–50; guides (gurus, teachers) and, 24–28, 79–82, 97–99; higher, as a state of unity, 8–9; increasing, 41–47ff.; interchange of methods and, 47–49; karma and reincarnation and, 141–67; levels (planes) of, 31–34, 131–37, 141–67; limits of knowing and, 51–54, 57–58, 117ff., 130, 144, 148ff., 157ff.; love as, 60, 152–54; mandala process and, 10–13; mantras and (*see* Mantras); meditation and (*see* Meditation); mind moments and, 114–16; nature of awareness and, 129–31; and nirvana, 115–16; one-pointedness of mind and, 93–97, 118–28, 145 (*see also* Centering); optimum being and, 85–89; and other forms of life, 170–71; path of, 1–6ff.; psychotherapy and, 20–21, 24–28; social responsibility and, 37–41
Consecration, 3, 4
Craving, 44, 126–28. *See also* Attachment(s); Desire(s)

Dance, evolution of consciousness as, 6, 8, 25, 42, 46–47ff., 51–53, 54, 58, 76

Death (dying), 24, 32–33, 59, 61–62, 113–14, 138, 156–57, 172, 173; karma and reincarnation and, 156–57, 158–67
Decisions, making of, 139
Depression, 61–62, 64, 79–80
Desire(s), 28, 29, 30, 44, 84–85, 124–27, 172–73 (*see also* Attachment[s]); connected with survival and reproduction, 167–70; for enlightenment, 172, 173; karma and reincarnation and, 141–67; transmission of energy of, 90–91
Despair, 79–80, 149–50
Devotion, 35
Dharma, 3, 142
Diet, 13, 65–68, 127. *See also* Food (eating)
Dr. Strange Comics, 46
Drop-outs, 94–95, 98–99
Drugs, use of, iii, 20–25, 31–32, 47–48, 58–59, 105. *See also* specific kinds
Dualisms, 31; surrender of, 173–74

Eating. *See* Food (eating)
Education (noneducation), 93–99; one-pointedness of mind and, 93–97; readiness for learning and, 94–97, 98; teachers as conveyors of the universe, 97–99
Ego, 17, 61, 76, 77, 92, 93, 98, 122–23, 154, 167–68 (*see also* Roles); control and, 29–30, 59; psychosis and, 72, 73–74; surrender of, 139, 165
Einstein, Albert, 38, 130
Energy, 4, 13, 19–20, 32–33, 40–41, 45, 60; centering and, 91–92; chakras, 28–31 (*see also* Chakras); *kalapas,* 114–15; raising the *Kundalini,* 20, 128–29; transmutation of, 13, 19–20, 84–85, 89–91; units of, 130–31, 135
English, distinctions between Sanskrit and, 10, 92–93
Enlightenment, 3, 20, 59–60; desire for, 172, 173
Esalen, 50, 77–78
Essences, 147, 150
Eternal present, 13. *See also* "Here and now" moment
Evolving consciousness, 6, 8, 25, 42, 46–47ff., 51, 53–54, 58, 76
Experiments (experimenters), 50–51

179

For the past decade, Ram Dass has been involved as a founder and board member in the work of the Seva Foundation—an organization dedicated to exploring compassionate action as a spiritual path. Seva assists people working to relieve suffering both in Third World countries and at home; its projects include free cataract surgery in India and Nepal, agricultural projects among Mayan villages in Guatemala, craft cooperatives for refugees in Mexico, and child health services for Native American peoples, as well as help for the homeless in the United States. Write to the Seva Foundation, 8 North San Pedro Road, San Rafael, California 94903 for further information about its programs.

Books, audiotapes, and videotapes by Ram Dass and other teachers can be obtained through the Hanuman Tape Library, P.O. Box 2320, Delray Beach, Florida 33447. The Tape Library offers a free catalog on request.